MW00986827

養生訓

YOJOKUN

Life Lessons from a Samurai

Kaibara Ekiken

TRANSLATION BY
William Scott Wilson

KODANSHA INTERNATIONAL
Tokyo • New York • London

CONTENTS

This translation is dedicated to
Dr. Noble Jonathan David
and to the memory of
Dr. Scottie Jackson Wilson

This book is presented as a translation of a classic
Japanese text and is not intended to replace medical
consultation and treatment. Please consult a doctor or other
appropriate health professionals for any problems you may
be having. Neither the translator nor the publisher may be
found liable for any adverse effects or consequences
resulting from the advice in this book.

Distributed in the United States by Kodansha America, LLC, and in
the United Kingdom and continental Europe by Kodansha Europe
Ltd. Published by Kodansha International Ltd., 17–14 Otowa 1-
chome, Bunkyo-ku, Tokyo 112–8652.

Preface, Introduction, and translation 2008 William Scott Wilson.
All rights reserved. Printed in Japan.
ISBN 978–4–7700–3077–1

First edition, 2008
18 17 16 15 14 13 12 11 10 09   10 9 8 7 6 5 4 3 2

Library of Congress Cataloging-in-Publication Data

Kaibara, Ekiken, 1630-1714.
    Yojokun: life lessons from a samurai/Kaibara Ekiken ; translated
by William Scott Wilson.
       p. cm.
    Includes bibliographical references and index.
    1. Self care, Health—Early works to 1800. 2. Health behavior—Early
works to 1800. 3. Hygiene—Early works to 1800. 4. Conduct of life—
Early works to 1800. I. Title.
    RA776.95.K2513 2009
    613—dc22
                                     2008027142

www.kodansha-intl.com

PREFACE

The true meaning of the term *bushido* (the Way of the Samurai) has long—and often heatedly—been debated in Japan. Even today, well-educated and informed masters of the various martial arts will strongly disagree about the nuances and the deeper significance of the term. Nevertheless, many would agree that *bushido* encompasses the concepts of sincerity, selflessness, a measure of cultural attainment, martial skills, and a willingness to die for one's cause. The argument for this last concept, the willingness to die, perhaps reached its apex of expression in the eighteenth-century work *Hagakure*, with its famous phrase, "The Way of the samurai is found in death." Although the death of the ego is emphasized in *Hagakure* as much as that of the physical body, the idea that the samurai's Way finds its meaning in his demise has suffused modern thinking about the subject.

For this reason, I was pleased to encounter a work of the same period that is almost a mirror image of *Hagakure*. In total contrast to a stance of *not* valuing one's own life, the author of this very different work emphasized that a strong body, mind, and spirit were essential to the warrior. He reasoned that a man in the military class would be unable to carry out his duties if he were enervated or lived a short life. "With the loss of your life," he wrote, "you are good for nothing," and he argued that to hasten one's own demise "is fundamentally stupid."

Over his long career, the author, a samurai doctor and philosopher known as Kaibara Ekiken, took notes on how a samurai might live a life of health in harmony with Nature, based on the maintenance of *ch'i*, and was concerned primarily with how *ch'i*, the very essence of life, is

7

affected by everyday activities such as eating, drinking, intimate relations, and even bathing. In Ekiken's eighty-fourth year, these notes were compiled as the *Yojokun* (Lessons on Nurturing Life). The book is a clear departure from other samurai-class writings. Rather than a treatise on sword techniques or philosophical discussions on the unity of Zen and the martial arts, its focus is on how to maintain the healthy physical and mental foundation upon which techniques and philosophy depend. Thus, "Taking care of your life is your first important work as a human being."

Although intended for the samurai class of his time, the *Yojokun* was soon in the hands of both rich and poor. It is still widely read today, and new editions in both modern and eighteenth-century Japanese appear regularly. It is translated here with the intention of broadening perspectives on warrior thought and of providing a historically esteemed health manual for those interested in traditional Oriental medicine. Omitted are sections concerning the specialized details on herbal drugs, acupuncture, and moxa, which would probably mean little to the modern reader.

The completion of any book project, no matter how minor, always depends on the help of a great many people. I would like to express my deep appreciation to my editor, Barry Lancet, for his unwavering encouragement and masterful editing of this work; to the entire staff at Kodansha International for their patience and care; to Ichikawa Takashi for supplying a number of editions of the *Yojokun* that had been unavailable to me; to Professor Laura Nenzi for her help with research materials; to Dr. Daniel Medvedov and Dr. Justin Newman for their invaluable advice and explanations concerning traditional Oriental medicine; to John Siscoe for his suggestions and encouragement; to my wife Emily for her patient reading of the manuscript and for making it far more readable; and to my late professors, Professor Hiraga Noboru and Dr. Richard McKinnon, without whose early guidance I would hardly have known where to start. Any and all mistakes are my own.

NOTE: I have included in the introduction a number of quotes from *The Yellow Emperor's Classic on Medicine* (Japanese, *Kotei Naikei Somon*; Chinese, *Huang Ti Nei Ching Su Wen*: 黄帝内経素門) which I thought would be interesting, informative, or a good summary of the matter being discussed. This book, probably written early in the first millennium B.C., was one of Ekiken's favorite sourcebooks, and remains primary reading for practitioners of Oriental medicine even today. Ekiken refers to this work—the title of which is often abbreviated as the *Sumon* or *Somon*—throughout the *Yojokun*, lamenting that many aspiring doctors of his time could not read the classical Chinese in which it is written. Ekiken was a keen observer, especially in matters of medical methodology, and would not reject facts, even if they contradicted revered texts. Nevertheless, his thinking was much influenced by this book, not only in terms of basic concepts, but also in the details of nurturing one's health.

Heaven's command is called one's nature.
Following one's nature is called the Way.
Practicing the Way is called learning.

Doctrine of the Mean

———————

Setting up our intention is at least half of
learning. It is like aiming at
a target with a bow and arrow.

Kaibara Ekiken

———————

If you hit the mark on the wrong target,
you have missed.

Fukuoka Masanobu

NOTE: Japanese and Chinese names in the text are given
in the traditional order, family name preceding given name.

———————

An abbreviated chart of Chinese dynasty dates may be
found at the back of the book.

INTRODUCTION

Lieh Yu-k'ou was showing off his skills at archery to Pai-hun Wu-jen.[1] He drew his bow to full strength and, with a bowl of water placed on his left elbow, released an arrow. As the arrow flew, he fitted another arrow and released it, and then yet another. During this time, he stood as still as a statue. He spilled not a drop of water.

Pai-hun Wu-jen said, "This is archery in which you shoot.[2] It is not archery in which you do not shoot. Let's climb a mountain, walk onto a teetering rock overlooking a pool a hundred fathoms deep, and see if you can still shoot."

With that, Pai-hun Wu-jen scaled a high mountain, strode over to an unstable rock overlooking a pool a hundred fathoms deep, and backed up until his heels hung over the edge. He then motioned Yu-k'ou to approach. Yu-k'ou lay down on the ground, with sweat flowing down to the bottoms of his feet, and crawled over.

Pai-hun Wu-jen said,

> *Now, the "man who has arrived"[3]*
> *Can look right up at the blue sky,*
> *Dive down into the Yellow Springs[4] below,*
> *Be shaken and battered in the eight directions,*
> *But his spirit and ch'i will not change.*

Then he looked at Lieh Yu-k'ou and said, "Now you shrink in fear and blink your eyes. Are you not in danger within?"

Lieh Tzu, Chapter 2[5]

This story illustrates that a martial artist must be able to manifest his skill under any circumstances, not just those that are favorable or convenient. Combat and confrontation are not restricted to the gym or training hall, and intense training and superb skill may not be enough.

The same applies to the layman in his daily life. Any number of situations—emergencies or moments requiring quick action—may call for a collected, balanced mind and body which, if not already established, may be difficult to assume suddenly. This gives credence to the old Zen phrase, "The everyday mind, this is the Way," and by extension, "The everyday mind, this is the *dojo.*"

We are not made up of mind alone. Thus the ideal of a balanced mind and a balanced body being interdependent may be on the mark after all. Those seeking improvement may ask, what was it that caused Lieh Yu-k'ou to collapse and break into a sweat? And how can I dispel the danger "within"?

Lieh Yu-k'ou's physical *ch'i* (energy) was clearly well disciplined and his art was superb. But Kaibara Ekiken's interpretation of the man's failure would most likely have been that, despite his physical skill, Yu-k'ou had neglected his mental and spiritual *ch'i*. Ekiken's prescription would no doubt have included true mindfulness of the phenomena of the world and developing an understanding that man's physical and spiritual nature exist both within and without. This he explains in simple language and a grandfatherly tone throughout the *Yojokun.*

The *Yojokun* is important because it provides a short and concise manual, not just for our physical health but also for our mental and spiritual health. In it Ekiken outlines practical methods for the regulation and balance of *ch'i*, as well as a detailed account of the appropriate mental and spiritual attitudes that will safeguard the practices we follow from sinking into superficiality. For example, equal time is given to diet, proper body movement, mental quiet, and a profound sense of gratitude to Heaven and Earth. All are to ensure the proper flow of *ch'i*, a reduction of stress, and a state of harmony with the world.

The insights of the book, then, illuminate both the internal and external aspects of our existence in the world and treat them as a harmonious whole. To those of us brought up in the Western scientific tradition of understanding the universe as being made of "things" that bear little relation to us, this is a fascinating perspective on our place in the world and our approach to the Way.

THE FOUNDATION

There are three concepts or philosophical assumptions common to both the account of Lieh Yu-k'ou's performance of archery and the *Yojokun*. These concepts are also fundamental tenets of traditional Oriental medicine/philosophy (often not considered separate studies) and so permeate Taoism, Confucianism, and areas as seemingly disparate as agriculture, the martial arts, and everyday life. Properly understood, they constitute a Way, and an understanding of this Way is pivotal to the life, health, and habits of every martial artist, tea master, craftsman, and common workaday human being, no matter what his practice. Kaibara Ekiken, the author of the *Yojokun*, considered a basic grasp of these premises and their application to everyday living as absolutely essential, for the samurai as well as the common man and woman.

Ch'i

> *All that has physical form is identical with* ch'i.
> Ch'eng I[6]

Although the various schools of Taoism and Confucianism endlessly dispute the details of its function and origin, they agree that *ch'i* (*ki* in Japanese) is the material force that constitutes and pervades the universe, the cosmic vital energy, or universal breath. This *ch'i* is sometimes described as a matter-energy, the very wellspring of life which manifests itself as everything from man to mountain to the air we breathe. In this way, it may not be so different from what modern science has discovered to be the foundation of subatomic particles, a material force constantly in motion.

Ch'i, then, is the essence of all physical form, physical energy, and spirit, and its particular manifestation depends on how heavy or light, opaque or clear, it has become. Condensing, it forms solid matter; evaporating, it becomes spirit or potential. Coming together, it takes the form of life; dispersing, it is perceived as death. In any manifestation, however, it is a field of energy, spontaneously and continuously in transformation. It is important to understand that Ekiken constantly defined our fundamental or preternatural health as basic or primordial *ch'i*.[7]

According to Oriental thought, *ch'i* moves in predictable patterns and this is evident in Nature in the passing of the seasons, the lives of plants and animals (including humans), the flowing of rivers and streams, and indeed all natural phenomena. A corollary is that it is unwise to send *ch'i* into inappropriate places or directions. An underlying principle of the *Yojokun*, and Chinese medicine in general, is that *ch'i* "wants" to flow naturally, and that there are ways of using the body and mind to ensure this natural flow.

Not surprisingly, the improper flow of *ch'i* gives rise to a number of conditions that can have negative consequences for our health. "Rising *ch'i*," for example, may result in high blood pressure, palpitations, or headaches; while "falling *ch'i*" may bring on the prolapse of internal organs. Another problem is "leaking *ch'i*," which, Ekiken explains, may occur through our senses and their nine orifices (mouth, eyes, ears, nostrils, anus, and urethra). People with leaking *ch'i* are said to have a dull look to the eyes and a less humane consciousness. However, when *ch'i* is contained and conserved within the body through various exercises, internal circulation, physical and mental balance, and human-heartedness[8] are engendered. Also affecting *ch'i* is an excess of human emotions, which Ekiken cites as anger-agitating *ch'i*, fear-dispersing *ch'i*, anxiety-binding *ch'i*, and so on. He argues that by drawing in the senses through meditation and practicing even-mindedness, our *ch'i* flows evenly and with maximum balance.

How we integrate our lives with the transformation and maintenance of *ch'i* in order to attain harmony with its natural flow, however, depends on some knowledge of the two basic manifestations of *ch'i*, and of how they differentiate into the myriad aspects of what we call "the real world."

Yin and Yang

The two basic modalities of *ch'i* are the yin—the passive female element—and the yang, the active male force. The character for yin (陰) originally indicated the dark and shaded side of a mountain, a place where the sunshine cannot reach. Thus, it symbolizes a hidden place or thing and is indicative of the peaceful, soft, stopped, or closed. Yin *ch'i* is considered to be the fundamental energy of the Earth, the descending, and death.

The yang (陽), on the other hand, indicates a rising sun, the sunny side of a mountain, and the sun itself. It symbolizes the moving, the hard, and the opening. It is considered to be the basic *ch'i* force of heaven, the ascending, and birth.

As yin and yang interact, they in turn give rise to the five *ch'i* modalities of water, fire, earth, wood, and metal, and from there transform themselves into all the patterns of the universe, from the four seasons to the very life of man. Nothing, therefore, is inconsequent of yin and yang, and their successive activities give form to the universe—or the Ten Thousand Things in Heaven and Earth[9]—and, indeed, bring into being the Tao or Way.[10]

Thus, we cannot exclude or separate ourselves from the workings of *ch'i* and its universal patterns. This is expressed clearly in *The Yellow Emperor's Classic on Medicine*,[11] the earliest Chinese manual on medicine, which was a basic text for Ekiken and remains primary reading for doctors of Oriental medicine even today:

> Listen, the four seasons and yin and yang are the foundations of all the Ten Thousand Things. Therefore, the sages nurtured their yang in the spring and summer, and their yin in the autumn and winter, in order to follow the very root of things. In this way, together with the Ten Thousand Things, they followed the natural rise and fall at the gate of life and growth.
>
> The person who goes against this root strikes at his very foundation and destroys its true force. Thus, yin and yang and the four seasons are the beginning and end of the Ten Thousand Things, and the foundation of life and death. Going against them gives birth to disaster, but following along with them means not giving rise to severe disease. This is called Obtaining the Way.

The "root" alluded to is the balanced flow of the two modalities of *ch'i*, and of all their permutations and combinations. The question, then, becomes one of understanding just exactly what this balance is and how it may be achieved.

Regulation

For this reason, closing the door is called Earth [the female, yin], opening the door is called Heaven [the male, yang], and their successive closing and opening is called transformation. Their various comings and goings are called intercourse, and their manifestation is called form. That which has physical form is called an object.[12] To control and use objects is called regulation.

I Ching, Ta Chuan (The Great Treatise)

According to circumstances, *ch'i* transforms now into yin, now into yang. Excessive transformation into the one, however, will lead to the pronounced formation of the other, resulting in either a disruption of natural rhythm or a rupture of the normal balance—both of which are demonstrated for us by Lieh Yu-k'ou's collapse. Regulation of yin and yang, then, is the key.

Whether stated explicitly or implicitly, one of the greatest concerns of Oriental philosophy is the preservation and maintenance of *ch'i*, which, as noted, in its innumerable manifestations of yin and yang, affects everything from the passing of the four seasons to our daily comings and goings. According to this view, our health (both spiritual and physical) and ability to act efficiently in the world depend entirely on how we conform to the environmental balance and rhythm manifested in Nature, and how we regulate and adjust our lives and habits—not only to seasonal changes, but also in being mindful of our drinking, eating, sexual activity, physical movement (or lack thereof), and even of the clothing we wear. Regulation, in such instances, means moderation, and it is in moderation that balance is found.

Ch'i, however, is manifested in both the phenomenal *and* the noumenal, and both Taoists and Confucians agree that the two cannot be thought of as separate entities. Thus, the Way is obtained not only through physical practice, but in the regulation of our human relations and emotional lives as well. This view will have been substantially affirmed in many of the works on Chinese medicine and philosophy Ekiken studied, and it is clearly explained in *The Yellow Emperor's Classic on Medicine*:

> If one is calm and at peace, and without disturbing thoughts, he will follow his true *ch'i* and maintain his nervous system within. How then will sickness enter in? In this way, one makes his will tranquil and his desires few; he puts his mind at ease and is without fear; he labors with his body, but does not become fatigued; and his *ch'i* follows along and is well regulated . . .

Thus, enjoying the flavor of his food and being content with his clothing, he is happy with what he is used to, and entertains no doubts about his situation. Such people are said to be without superficialities. In this way, greed cannot distract them, nor can they be deluded by the lewd and lascivious. And they will fear nothing, whether they are dull or clever, intelligent or lacking. Thus they will be in harmony with the Way.

An underlying tenet of regulation—the regulation of yin and yang in all of their aspects—is that you cannot live an unbalanced emotional or ethical life and simultaneously have a balanced health and practice, be that practice in the martial arts, the tea ceremony, or everyday office life. And, if we believe we can exclude ourselves from regulating either the grosser or the subtler workings of *ch'i* and its universal patterns, then we, like Lieh Yu-k'ou, may be in for a rough ride.

THE *YOJOKUN*

The *Yojokun* (literally, Lessons on Nurturing Life) is the culmination of over six decades of observation on how a human being may remain vigorous and healthy throughout life and live to old age in a satisfying and fulfilling manner. The book is, in a sense, Ekiken's last will and testament to the samurai class, as it was completed shortly before he passed away.

A practicing physician, Ekiken was a keen observer of people and their surroundings and had ample opportunities to examine the physical and psychological condition of his fellow warriors and their families. As a botanist, he had first-hand experience with the herbs used as medicines in his day (and today), as well as their properties and efficacy.

The main thrust of this book, however, is not medicines and cures, but a lifestyle that prevents the onset of disease. In this, too, Ekiken followed the path laid out by *The Yellow Emperor's Classic on Medicine*:

The sages did not treat those who were already ill; they treated those who were not yet ill. They did not regulate that which was already in chaos; they regulated that which was not yet in disorder. Listen, this is what health and balance is all about.

Ekiken took a holistic view of health. His perspective encompassed not only the threat of disease, but also the circumstances surrounding one's daily habits, activities, and frame of mind. In this sense, it may be said that Ekiken was ahead of his time.

Ekiken specifically premised his book and his medical practice on the understanding that good health is based on a vigorous *ch'i*, the balance of yin and yang, and how the latter two are regulated. The book is not, however, a simple statement of philosophical ideas, but rather an extensive set of notes on how this goal may be reached. Following are some of the fundamental concepts that form the bedrock of this work.

Awareness

One of the most important aspects in the practice of any art—whether the martial arts, the art of tea, or Noh—is awareness, and this is given primary importance in the *Yojokun*. Ekiken explains repeatedly that we must be aware of the negative influences to our health both in the environment (excesses of heat, cold, wind, and humidity) and in our emotions (excesses of joy, hatred, depression, and so on).

These negative factors are to be regarded as opponents or enemies. We must be no less aware of them than a swordsman is of well-armed opponents surrounding him. Such deep awareness to circumstances—both external and internal—is strongly advocated by both military strategists and civilian Confucian philosophers.

Ekiken extended this idea. He realized that we are often unaware of the things that can harm us, and so enjoined us to develop an awareness of the world (external and internal) and become more deeply respectful of the effects that it can have on our health.

Movement

The Sino-Japanese characters for "animal"—among which we humans number—are 動物, meaning "moving thing." Understanding that this name describes our fundamental nature, Ekiken encouraged his patients to move about as often as possible or practical.

With the cessation of military activities and the samurai taking on more sedentary clerical duties, he saw the growing inactivity among the warrior class and detected a concomitant listlessness, lack of purpose, and loss of health. He reasoned that as *ch'i* is the very foundation of our health, its circulation should be paramount. Throughout the *Yojokun*, he emphasizes that inactivity must be countered with activity in order to encourage the flow of *ch'i* and prevent its stagnation. Although Ekiken consistently promotes balance, his attitude is that if you can't walk, then stand; if you can't stand, then sit; but worst of all is lying down.

Preventative Practice

Listen, treating a disease that has already developed, or trying to bring order to disruptions that has already begun, is like digging a well after you've become thirsty, or making weapons after the battle is over. Wouldn't it already be too late?

The Yellow Emperor's Classic on Medicine

According to Ekiken, medicine, acupuncture, moxa treatment, and hot springs (the major treatments of the time) are all methods of last resort. The greater part of staying healthy can be accomplished with preventative practices involving, first, a correct physical and emotional life, and, second, maintaining an awareness of the surrounding environment.

Disease, Ekiken says, is hard to cure and requires heroic measures that are painful besides. Being circumspect beforehand and doing everything possible to avoid the onset of illness is a much wiser strategy. He likens his preventative measures for health to the classical strategies of warfare. In the *Yojokun*, he writes:

> Sun Tzu[13] said, "The man who uses his army well performs no outstanding meritorious deeds." In other words, the man who skillfully puts his army's resources in play appears, from the outside, to be doing very little at all. Why? Because he defeats the enemy before the battle ever begins. Sun Tzu further said, "The ancients who were skillful at defeating the enemy were those who defeated the easily defeated."

Restraint

For Ekiken, restraint is the key to preventative practice. He repeatedly declares that excess and the thoughtless giving in to desire are the portals to later disaster. The correct strategy, he says, is a deep respect for the dangers of careless indulgence in eating, drinking, sexual activity, work, and even rest. The foundation of his strategy is the clear understanding that an excess of yin will inevitably become yang, and an excess of yang will inevitably become yin.

Similarly, a few millennia before Ekiken's time, the author of *The Yellow Emperor's Classic on Medicine* focused on lack of restraint:

> In the remote past, those who understood the Way followed the patterns of yin and yang, harmonized these with nurturing practices, put limits on their eating and drinking, and did not recklessly overexert themselves. Thus, body and spirit interacted well, they lived out their naturally given years, and only left this world after a hundred years or more.

People these days are not like this. They drink wine as though it were berry juice, make arbitrary what should be constant, get drunk and indulge in sex, deplete their pure essence because of desire, and thus suffer a loss of their fundamental health. They do not understand how to maintain their essential *ch'i* and constantly push their nervous system to excess. Doing this to make their hearts happy, they run counter to the true enjoyment of life, and wake and sleep without regulation. Thus they fizzle out after fifty years or so.

Drugs and Medicine

Ekiken understood disease to be a loss of balance between the yin and yang of the physical body, regardless of its immediate or external cause. He further understood that once a disease is in progress, medicines or other treatments such as acupuncture or moxa might be necessary to fight the illness in what he calls the "battlefield" of the body.

What Ekiken further brings to our attention in the *Yojokun* is that drugs, herbs, and other treatments all use a distorted or unbalanced substance or condition to counter the distorted, out-of-balance nature of the disease. Any medicine, therefore, is to be considered only with extreme caution. For example, taking drugs that are not called for, or receiving acupuncture when it is not really required, can be a dangerous matter, as the internal condition of the body will be distorted without cause. The same restraint must be applied to herbs and other drugs that enhance sexual potency, and even to supplementary herbs (such as vitamins) to increase energy or "good health."

As in other aspects of health, Ekiken advocated a balanced diet (less food is better) as the best preventative medicine. If supplementary nutrition is required, it should be derived from everyday natural foods. He understood that some foods are more yin than yang, and vice versa, and advocated circumspection in what we eat and when. Even herbs like ginseng he recognized as potent enough to cure an imbalance, and strong enough to cause a similar imbalance if the body was already in good health. If inappropriate food can harm the body, how much more so can inappropriate medicines, herbs, and hot springs treatments?

All foods and drugs consist of a balance or potency of *ch'i* that affects our own *ch'i*. Ekiken would agree that "we are what we eat," and he advocates proper caution and restraint in what we choose to take into our bodies.

Emotions

Heaven has provided the four seasons and the Five Elements [wood, fire, earth, metal, and water], and by these it gives birth, develops, reaps, and stores away, and [also] creates cold, heat, drought, humidity, and wind. Man has five organs [the liver, heart, spleen, lungs, and kidneys] that give birth [respectively] to anger, joy, worry, grief, and fear. Thus, joy and anger can harm *ch'i*, as cold and heat may harm our physical form. Violent anger may harm our yin, and excessive joy may harm our yang.... When joy and anger are without restraint, it can be likened to times when heat and cold become excessive and life is not secure.

The Yellow Emperor's Classic on Medicine

In the *Yojokun*, Ekiken deals not just with anger and joy but also with the entire gamut of our emotions, noting that an ongoing excess of a negative or positive emotion will result in physical discomfort or worse. To ensure mental equilibrium and to stay in accord with the Way, he prescribes the giving up of envy and greed, and the development of contentment with one's lot. This does not mean that one should not feel these emotions—being human, we feel them naturally. It is the *excess* of emotions (and the accompanying overstimulation of their corresponding organs) that he warns against. Elsewhere Ekiken writes on the correct balance of an emotional response:

For a good mental balance, our emotions should be appropriate, neither excessive nor insufficient, and undistorted. Be happy when you should be happy, but do not go overboard. Be angry when you should be angry, but do not take your anger to extremes. The other emotions should be regulated in like manner.

Yamato Zokkun, Chapter 3

In recent years research has increasingly indicated that long-term depression may be connected with the onset of heart disease, and that ongoing excessive anger or stress may lead to high blood pressure and its accompanying complications. In light of this, the importance Ekiken placed on a balanced and moderate emotional life seems to have been justified.

The same obviously applies to the practitioner of any art, as excessive or strong emotions are anathema to concentration, coordination, and perception. Ekiken understood this and equated a balanced emotional life not only with health but also with the virtue of the samurai class itself.

Gratitude

It may appear strange that Ekiken prescribed a sense of gratitude as promoting good health, but he began a number of his writings, including the *Yojokun*, with that proposal. Gratitude, after all, precludes envy and greed, promotes a sense of contentment, offers a cure for anger and resentment, and perhaps provides an incentive to moderation, restraint, and balance.

Ekiken recommends that we engender a strong sense of gratitude, not only to our parents, without whom we would not exist, but to Nature itself,[14] which provides us with the material for our food and clothing, the joy of the four seasons, and the very air we breathe. For his own class, it went without saying that the samurai should feel immense gratitude toward his feudal lord, who supplied him with the stipend necessary to live, and to the other classes lower in the social hierarchy, who provided him with so many goods.

Thus we end at the beginning: good health is what you owe to yourself, but even more so to the world around you. In Ekiken's view, to act irresponsibly and to spoil or injure your health through neglect or excess is the greatest ingratitude to the parents who gave you birth, to the society that educated and provided for you, as well as to the Heaven and Earth that make all life possible.

A brief note should be added about the style in which the *Yojokun* was written. Although Ekiken ostensibly wrote this book for the warrior class, it has been noted that he had strong empathy for the lower classes, and he probably intended the book for them as well. Thus he made some effort to write the work in relatively simple Japanese so that anyone with some education could understand it. Indeed, the *Yojokun* seems to have made its way into the hands of people of all classes and became a handbook for good health even for those people who could not afford a doctor.[15] For the same reason, perhaps, there are repetitions throughout the work, ensuring that the reader will not miss the most important points or fail to see how certain methods would work in different situations.

In the end, it is a writing style that reflected Ekiken's human-heartedness, the highest Confucian ideal of benevolence, based on the concept that man lives always among others and should treat them as he would have them treat him.

KAIBARA EKIKEN

Kaibara Ekiken was one of the preeminent intellectuals of his time. A samurai who trained in the martial arts of the sword, bow, and spear, as well as horsemanship, he was also a practicing physician and a lecturer on the philosophy of Confucianism. Ekiken was born in Fukuoka Castle on the southern island of Kyushu in 1630, thirty years after the history-altering battle at Sekigahara and eight years before the Shimabara Rebellion, the last significant conflict of the samurai era. Thus, although his paternal grandfather had performed meritorious deeds in battle while serving Takeda Shingen and later as a samurai of the Kuroda clan, and his father and elder brother participated in the action at Shimabara, Ekiken himself would become a samurai of the new world of the Tokugawa shogunate—an era of peace in which the warrior had to adjust to a world without war. Ekiken would fare far better than others in this adjustment and become an ideal samurai of the new age.

Ekiken was a somewhat delicate child and was encouraged by his father, also a physician, to study medicine and nutrition from the age of thirteen. From the same time, he was taught both medicine and Confucian philosophy under the tutelage of his older brother Sonzai, for whom he had the greatest respect. Thus, from the very beginning, Ekiken studied medicine—caring for and curing the sick and ailing—and Confucianism, which places its highest value on human-heartedness, which in great part means helping others. The associated values would guide Ekiken throughout his life, along with his great love and respect for Nature, a legacy, perhaps, of his Shinto priest ancestors.[16]

During his time, Ekiken was most famous as a scholar of Confucianism, about which he wrote extensively. He was a highly respected lecturer on this subject—one of the major studies suggested by the shogunate for the samurai class—and traveled widely, giving talks and tutoring not only other scholars but also the heirs to the Kuroda clan and members of the Tokugawa shogunate itself.

Ekiken's curiosity about the world was insatiable, and along with his interest in Confucianism, he studied subjects as varied as botany, agriculture, topography, astronomy, the *I Ching* (an understanding of which he declared necessary for the practice of medicine), zoology, linguistics, mathematics, and military tactics, to name just a few. He was also a prolific writer, somehow finding the time between his medical practice, lecturing, study, and travel to write over a hundred volumes. His book on the topography of Chikuzen Province (now part of Fukuoka Prefecture), which took him fifteen years in research and writing, is still studied today by scholars of that subject. In his *Yamato Honzo* (Plants of Japan), he classified and gave detailed descriptions of over 1,500 plants, birds, and other animals.

To gain such extensive knowledge, Ekiken both traveled widely and made the acquaintance of some of the finest scholars of his day. In fact, he made at least twelve journeys to the capital of Edo (now Tokyo), traveling by sea, on horse, and on foot; took a great number of trips to Kyoto; and extensively explored his home province of Chikuzen. Nor was this the extent of his travels, as can be seen by the titles of his numerous travelogues on such places as northwestern Japan, Nikko, the Kiso Road, Ariyama, and Japan in general.

During these journeys, Ekiken met, befriended, and engaged the greatest scholars of the day in friendly debate on a wide variety of subjects. He also took the time and had the interest to talk with farmers, artisans, and people of the common classes in general, listening to their "most insane utterances," but never dismissing anything out of hand. Brought up in part by commoners after his mother and stepmother died, he was aware of their practical experiences and wisdom, and lent his ear to both high- and lowborn.

Ekiken was motivated by an altruistic love for all creatures and things, and a desire to help them in a practical way. His wide range of studies focused more on *jitsugaku*, or practical learning, than simply on study for its own sake. And in this connection, it is important to note that a large number of his works were *kun*—precepts or lessons—on subjects as diverse as the proper understanding of what it means to be a warrior and how to truly be content and enjoy life. One of his very last books, the *Yojokun* is testimony to both his concern for his fellow human beings and the practical steps by which they might lead healthier lives.

At the age of thirty-eight, Ekiken married Esaki Token, the seventeen-year-old daughter of a local samurai administrator. Token is said to have been talented in music, calligraphy, and poetry, and to have studied enough history and philosophy to keep Ekiken on his toes. Indeed, one of his books, *Onna Daigaku*, or Greater Learning for Women, is speculated to have been written by Token but published under Ekiken's name to give the work his cachet and thus a wider readership. Token and Ekiken seem to have been a very happy couple. She often accompanied him on his travels, discussed with him the subjects he pursued, and was a great companion and comfort to him in his old age. When she died at the age of sixty-two, he finished up his compilation of the *Yojokun* and two other works, and passed away the following year.

All indications are that Ekiken was an affable and engaging man and a sympathetic listener with a quick mind. He seems to have genuinely held all classes of people and both sexes in deep respect, not a requisite quality of a member of the ruling samurai class. In spite of having written nearly a library of books, Ekiken was as at home tramping through the fields observing the flora and fauna of Japan as he was in his own study. In his book *Rakkun* (Lessons for Contentment), he extols the active appreciation of the four seasons and of the flowers, trees, and animals.

In the end, we can perhaps best envision Ekiken at a patient's bedside, his manner friendly and sympathetic, explaining the problem, prescribing a cure, and adding a small dose of philosophy just for good measure.

CONCLUSION

It should be noted that the kind of medicine practiced four hundred years ago by Kaibara Ekiken is still being practiced in Japan today and—with local differences—on the Korean peninsula, in China, and in other traditional Oriental societies. This is apparently not because of the inertia of tradition or because of cost considerations (it is not inexpensive), but because it is effective.

In Japan there exist the most modern Western-style medical facilities to be found anywhere *and* traditional *kanpoyaku* (Chinese herbal medicine) clinics in the same neighborhoods. People will visit one or the other according to their particular ailment. For pyorrhea one may visit a modern dentist; for a skin disorder, a traditional doctor of Oriental medicine. Nor are the traditional clinics and doctors restricted to the Far East. Doctors practicing *kanpoyaku* can be found in growing numbers across North America and Europe, and treatments are increasingly covered even under the most conservative insurance plans.

Modern medicine is increasingly finding value in the preventative measures advocated by practitioners of Oriental medicine in general and by Ekiken in particular: one thinks immediately of proper diet, exercise, and the restraint of anger and other strong emotions, just for starters. In another arena, self-help books and gurus now advocate the virtues of moderation and circumspection to help control our mental and emotional lives.

The *Yojokun*, then, is not just a quaint vestige of Orientalia, but a living guide to a traditional Way to live and maintain a balanced health. If we do not immediately understand some of its more exotic prescripts, it may be wiser not to dismiss them outright, but to approach the work as Ekiken himself might have: with humility, curiosity, respect, and imagination.

The Way of
Nurturing Life

General Remarks

You should consider the foundation of your body to be your father and mother, and its beginning to be Heaven and Earth. As you are born and then nourished by Heaven and Earth and your father and mother, you cannot truly consider your body a personal possession with which you can do as you choose. Rather, your body is a treasured gift from Heaven and Earth. It is also something left to you by your parents. Thus, you should cherish it, nourish it, neither damage nor destroy it, and take care of it for the natural span of its life. This is the basis of being dutiful to Heaven and Earth and to your father and mother.

Should you lose your body, you are good for nothing. Further, to damage or destroy it thoughtlessly is the highest ingratitude. Indeed, to consider the gift of life as your possession alone and then to abuse it by overindulging in food, drink, sex, or in any other manner is to squander your health and invite disease to enter. To hasten your own demise so thoughtlessly demonstrates extreme ingratitude. It also suggests a fundamental ignorance.

Once born into the world, you can lead a long, happy, and enjoyable life if you are intently respectful of your father and mother and Heaven and Earth, and if you walk the path of morality and compliance with duty. Isn't such a life what everyone truly desires?

If this is what you seek, you must first consider the above-mentioned new Way in which to look at life, learn the techniques of the Way of Nurturing Life discussed in these pages, and regulate your body well.

These are the very first rules in human life.

2

There is nothing more precious than the human body. Would you trade it for anything else under Heaven or within the Four Seas? To remain unaware of the techniques for taking care of it and arbitrarily give in to indulgences that would destroy it would be the height of stupidity.

Consider the relative importance of human life and of human desires. Every day, be careful with your health on that one day. If you fear the dangers of succumbing to selfish desires, the same way you fear walking on thin ice, you should live a long life and be able to avoid disaster.

Why shouldn't you enjoy life? You should. But even with all the wealth under Heaven and within the Four Seas, it will do you no good if life is short. Indeed, you may pile up a mountain of treasures, but it will be of no use. Thus, there is no greater fortune than following the Way of Nurturing Life, taking care of your body, and living a long life. For this reason, a long life is considered to be the first of the Five Happinesses listed in the *Book of Documents*.[1] It is, in fact, the very root of the Ten Thousand Happinesses.[2]

3

In all things, if you are unendingly diligent, you will undoubtedly see an effect. For example, if you plant seeds in the spring and nurture the seedlings in the summer, surely there will be a large harvest in the fall.

Similarly, if you make an effort to increase your understanding of how to care for your health and continue to do so for some time, you will definitely see effects: your body will become stronger, you will be free of disease, you will not only maintain your natural lifespan but lengthen it, and you will enjoy your life. You should not doubt this principle.

4

A person who loves his garden will tend it day and night, watering the plants, laying down mulch, fertilizing the soil, and eliminating pests. When the garden flourishes he will rejoice. When it declines he will grieve. Compared to your body, your garden is a trivial matter. How can you not love your body as much as the grasses and trees in your garden?

When you tend to your body and practice principles for nurturing your health with diligence, you are being dutiful to your parents as well as to Heaven and Earth. You are fulfilling your obligations to them. If you would do this for the sake of providing yourself with a long, happy life, you must temporarily put aside work that is not pressing and learn these techniques from the time you are young. Being circumspect with your body and taking care of your life is the most important work you have as a human being.

5

The first principle of the Way of Nurturing Life is avoiding overexposure to things that can damage your body. These can be divided into two categories: inner desires and negative external influences.

INNER DESIRES encompass the desires for food, drink, sex, sleep, and excessive talking, as well as the desires of the seven emotions—joy, anger, anxiety, yearning, sorrow, fear, and astonishment.

The **NEGATIVE EXTERNAL INFLUENCES** comprise the four dispositions of Nature: wind, cold, heat, and humidity.

If you restrain the inner desires, they will diminish.

If you are aware of the negative external influences and their effects, you can keep them at bay.

Following both of these rules of thumb, you will avoid damaging your health, be free from disease, and be able to maintain and even increase your natural lifespan.

6

Controlling your inner desires is the foundation of the Way of Nurturing Life. If you build a solid foundation, your natural strength will increase and you will be able to hold off negative exterior influences. If you are not circumspect with your inner desires and your health weakens, you will be easily worn down by the negative external influences, which could result in a serious illness and a shortening of your life.

By and large, the stipulations for CONTROLLING YOUR INNER DESIRES include the following:

+ You should eat and drink moderately, avoiding excess.
+ You should not eat food that might possibly damage your stomach and intestines, thus making you sick.
+ You should be careful with sexual desire, valuing your essential energy.
+ You should caution yourself about sleeping for long periods of time; you should not lie down at inappropriate times.
+ You should not sit at ease for long periods.
+ From time to time you should move your body and CIRCULATE YOUR CH'I. Especially after eating, you should take a walk of several hundred steps. If you sit leisurely for a long time, sit still after a meal, or quickly lie down to sleep before digesting your food, you will become stopped up inside and bring on disease. If you persist in any of these forms of inaction for a lengthy period of time, you will be unable to generate your own fundamental *ch'i* and you will become weak.
+ You should always be unwilling to diminish your health. Be sparing with your words and be moderate with the seven emotions, doing

your best to diminish the emotions of anger, sorrow, anxiety, and yearning.

+ If you are moderate in your desires, keep your mind level, keep your *ch'i* gentle and without violence, and remain quiet and unflustered, then your mind should always be at peace and harmonious. Neither will you be troubled or distressed.

These are the techniques for moderating your inner emotions and nurturing your fundamental health. *They are all components of the Way of Nurturing Life* and are discussed in further detail in other entries.

In addition, you should constantly protect yourself from the negative external influences of wind, cold, heat, and humidity.

Taking care of yourself revolves largely around being careful with both the interior and exterior.

Observe these points with great care.

7

Almost everyone is gifted with a long natural lifespan at birth. Those given a short lifespan are rare. Nevertheless, there are many people who, although healthy by nature and strong of body, are ignorant of the techniques of nurturing their health. Morning and night such people damage their fundamental health. Morning and night they unknowingly decrease their essential energy. The end result is that they depart this world early.

On the other hand, there are others who, despite being born with weak constitutions and prone to disease, learn to be circumspect and careful precisely because of their misfortune. Their awareness leads to a preservation of health and long life.

You can see these two types of people all around you and so should harbor no doubts about what I am saying.

Overindulging in your desires and damaging your body is the same as taking up a sword and killing yourself. One happens quickly while the other happens in increments, but the results are the same.

8

Lao Tzu noted that "a person's life lies within, not with Heaven."

Whether your life is long or short depends upon how your mind[3] will have it. Even people born with strong bodies and the potential for a long life will die young should they neglect to cultivate techniques for taking care of themselves. And those who are born at a disadvantage, with a weak body and a potentially stunted lifespan, can live long lives if they take care of themselves.

In other words, the fate of our health, and thus our lifespan, lies in our hands, not Heaven's. At birth, Nature deals out exceedingly short lifespans to only a few people. Men like Yen Tzu[4] are the exception.

9

There are principles by which you may extend your life. If one stokes the embers of a fire buried in the hearth, they will remain alive for a long time. Expose those embers to wind and they will soon die. In the same way, if you expose a tangerine to the elements, it will not last the year; but if you store it carefully and watch it well, it may be kept for a longer period than you might expect.

10

Your fundamental health is, in its origin, the *ch'i* that gives birth to all the Ten Thousand Things in Heaven and Earth.[5] If you do not have this *ch'i*, you will not be born. After you are born, you are aided by such external elements as food and drink, clothing and shelter. Thus, your fundamental health is provided for and your life stays on a steady course.

If you use external elements such as food and drink—which are to nourish your fundamental health—lightly, and do not eat or drink to excess, they will nourish your fundamental health, maintain your natural lifespan, and even lengthen your life. But if you use these elements to excess, your health will deteriorate and you will become sick. If you become seriously ill and exhaust your fundamental health, you will die. In the same way, if you give grasses and trees in your garden too much water or fertilizer, they will lose their vitality and wither away.

Thus, you should seek pleasure in your mind alone, and use external nourishment like food and drink lightly.

11

When taking care of your health, it is best to first NOURISH YOUR MIND AND CH'I. The essentials of this are as follows:

+ Suppress anger and desire.
+ Diminish grief and yearning.
+ Neither trouble your mind nor damage your *ch'i*.
+ Do not take excessive pleasure in sleep. If you sleep for long periods of time, your *ch'i* will stagnate and not circulate well.
+ Do not go to bed before digesting what you have eaten and drunk. To do so stifles your breathing and is injurious to your health. Please guard against this.
+ With alcoholic beverages, it is acceptable to become lightly drunk, but you should stop halfway. Avoid complete drunkenness.
+ With food, stop halfway to satiety, as it is not good to be completely full.
+ Establish limits with both food and drink and do not go beyond moderation.

+ Be circumspect with sexual desire from the time you are young. You must not be wasteful of your essential energy. If you use too much of this essential energy, your subordinate *ch'i* will be weakened, you will eradicate the very root of your fundamental health, and your life will surely be shortened.

If you cannot be circumspect with your food, drink, and sexual desire, you might end up using restorative medicines every day and supplementing your diet, but such efforts are likely to be of no use.

There are other actions or precautions to be taken:

+ You should watch out for exposure to and guard against the negative external influences of wind, cold, heat, and humidity.
+ Be moderate and prudent about conduct that requires standing for a long time. Move your body and take walks after eating.
+ Follow the Taoist health practices of stretching the joints and massaging the skin from time to time.
+ Stroke your hips and belly.
+ Exercise your hands and feet and thus circulate invigorated blood.
+ Allow your food to be digested before taking a nap or retiring for the night.
+ Never sit in one place for a long time.

All of these are very important for good health.

Success lies in safeguarding your health when you are *not* sick. Using medicine once you have become ill and attacking that illness with such treatments as acupuncture and moxa cautery are fallback measures and low on the scale of useful techniques for attending to your health.

You must make great efforts in regard to these matters.

The ears hear, the eyes see, the mouth eats and drinks, and the body enjoys sex. Each part of your body has a desire of its own liking. These are called appetites. When you have no self-control over your appetites and latch onto pleasures with greedy abandon, you will exceed your natural limits, damage your body, and thus exhibit a lack of common decency.[6]

All evil stems from doing whatever you like vis-à-vis your desires. Practicing self-control can defeat runaway desires. Good influences surface when you show self-control. Therefore, self-control and overindulging are, respectively, the foundations of good and evil. For this reason, in order to properly apply the techniques of the Way of Nurturing Life, you must be fully aware of and learn to control your desires.

In short, cast out *self-indulgence* and safeguard *forbearance*.

The negative external influences—wind, cold, heat, and humidity—are all weather related. Accidental exposure can lead to illness and death and is a matter of Heaven's decree, from which even sages and wise men cannot escape. However, if your inner *ch'i* is replete and you take solid preventative measures, succumbing to external influences will be rare. Illness due to personal excesses with food and drink is your own doing, not Heaven's decree.

Not to take steps to curb negative external influences shows negligence.

Not to develop self-control over your inner desires is an error on your part.

All negligence and errors occur simply as a result of not being careful.

14

In protecting your health, one single word rules supreme. If you put this word into action, you will live long and avoid illness. You will be dutiful to your parents, loyal to your lord. And you will support your clan and preserve your body. No matter what you do, you will not be mistaken.

What is this word?

It is *respect*.[7]

Having respect builds mental stamina for protecting your body. Respect as in paying attention to each and every thing, in not letting your *ch'i* move willfully, and in conducting yourself so as to make no mistakes. It is in constantly respecting the Way of Heaven and following it with circumspection. It is in fearing an overindulgence in human desires and so being prudent and maintaining self-control.

Respect is the starting point of circumspection. When you have respect, circumspection is born. Because of this, in his later years Chu Hsi[8] talked about the word *reverence*, it being close in meaning to *respect*.

15

There are two things that can interfere with taking care of yourself. One is a decline in your fundamental health, the other is its stagnation. Excessive eating, drinking, sexual activity, and exercise can lead to the latter. Both will damage your health.

16

The mind is the master of the body. You must make this master peaceful and calm.

The body is the servant of the mind. You must make it move and work.

When the mind is tranquil, it is replete. It is joyful and without pain.

When your body moves and works, food and drink move through it smoothly, your blood circulates well, and illness is kept at bay.

17

Generally speaking, using medicine, acupuncture, and moxa cautery are poor strategies of the last resort. If you 1) are moderate with food, drink, and sex, 2) establish times for sleeping and waking, and 3) take good care of yourself, you will not become ill.

Let's say that your stomach is obstructed, even though you are not a person inclined toward heavy drinking. If you take walks and work your body morning and night and do your best not to sit continually or sleep for long periods of time, you will not need to worry about the ongoing obstruction of your stomach. It will correct itself without the use of medicine, acupuncture, or moxa. This is the best strategy.

Medicines are all based on influencing the *ch'i*. Even medicines like *ninjin*, *ougi*, *byakujutsu*, and *kanzo*,[9] if not matched to the correct illness, can cause damage. Moreover, medicines of middling or poor quality can damage your fundamental health and open the door to other diseases.

Acupuncture can eliminate excessive *ch'i* but cannot supplement insufficient *ch'i*. If acupuncture is not fitting for the ailment in question, it can diminish your health. If moxa cautery is indiscriminately applied, it can raise your *ch'i* to inappropriate levels.

Medicine, acupuncture, and moxa cautery are, then, treatments with advantages and disadvantages. You should avoid them unless they become absolutely necessary. You should depend principally on preventative measures to insure your health.

The educated gentlemen[10] of the past enjoyed proper manners and put them into practice. They studied archery and horseback riding, put their strength to work, and practiced music, dance, and poetry recitation.[11] They nurtured their circulation, restricted their appetites, stabilized their minds and *ch'i*, and carefully protected themselves against negative external influences.

The educated gentleman's activities focused on the root rather than the branches, which is the highest strategy.

If you conduct yourself in the same way, illness will remain a stranger.

People often become sick because they do not understand the Way of Nurturing Life. Once they become sick, they drink medicine, order painful acupuncture, and apply hot moxa. They apply fire or needles, injuring the body their parents gave them. In a search for a cure, they attack themselves. They are reaching for the most distant branch rather than the root, which is a poor strategy.

If a ruler uses virtue to govern a country, the people will be obedient of themselves, no rebellions will occur, and there will be no need to attack or suppress them. Neglecting your body's basic health can be likened to a ruler neglecting the needs of his constituency. The subjects will grow discontent and revolt. Calling out the army to quell the unrest will not solve the root problem, only suppress it. Even if you fight and win a hundred times, this is not an admirable course of action. Neither is depending on medicines, acupuncture, and moxa when your body rebels. An admirable ruler will be virtuous and take care of his subjects. An admirable person will show respect for his body and take care of it.

19

You should put your body to work bit by bit every day. You should not sit in a relaxed position for a long time.

Every day, walk a few hundred paces in your garden after eating. Do this without fail. In rainy weather you can walk slowly around your room a number of times.

If you exercise like this daily and watch what you eat and drink, your vigor will not become obstructed and you will not become ill, even without the use of medicines or other treatment, and your life will be comfortable and happy.

20

Our bodies have a limited lifespan of one hundred years. Longevity at its best is one hundred years; at its middle, eighty years; and at its lowest, sixty. But there are few who make it to even sixty, and many others who succumb before fifty.

Why are people's lives so short? Because they do not understand the techniques of the Way of Nurturing Life. Or, simply put, the techniques of taking care of themselves.

Short lives are not a given. Longevity is. Unfortunately, nine out of ten people do damage to themselves. If you thoroughly understand the Way of Nurturing Life, you can live a long time.

21

Until a man reaches the age of fifty, his vigor has not settled and his wisdom has not matured. He is still unacquainted with the past and present and has not become accustomed to society's changes. The words that he speaks are often mistaken, and he has many regrets about his actions. Nor does he know the pleasures of the truths of human life.

Dying before the age of fifty is said to be a calamity. The phrase "an unfortunately short life" is also an accurate reflection. If you live a long life, you will have many pleasures and many advantages. Day by day, you understand things that you didn't understand before the age of fifty. Month by month, you are able to do more things that were previously beyond your ability. Thus, to advance in learning and to develop your knowledge is impossible without a long life. For this reason, you must practice the techniques found in the Way of Nurturing Life and, no matter what, seek to extend your life beyond fifty. If you are able to do this, you will enjoy the additional fruits of longevity mentioned here.

22

The men of ancient times stated that there are techniques for living a long life. They declared that "a person's life lies within himself, not within Heaven." Thus, if you are deeply resolved to practice these techniques, a long life is a matter of your own efforts.

You should not doubt this.

However, if your *ch'i* is violent, if you let your desires run rampant, and if you are not circumspect, you will be unable to live a long life.

23

Generally speaking, the human body is weak and transient. It is like a lamp in the wind, a precarious thing that is easily blown out. Treat your body as a matter of great importance.

A great number of enemies attack your body from within and from without, so you must give the matter great attention. All of the previously mentioned desires and emotions—the internal enemies—arise from within your own body and will attack. They can be truly frightening.

Wind, cold, heat, and humidity—the external enemies—present entirely different threats. Forged of neither metal nor stone, the human body will easily succumb to strong external forces if not protected.

You preserve your constitution by knowing the correct techniques for protecting yourself. Even if you were born with a naturally strong *ch'i*, if you do not practice the Way of Nurturing Life you will fall prey to your natural enemies just as a general who is lacking in wisdom and knowledge of military tactics, will fall to defeat.

To defeat internal enemies, you must make your heart strong and use patience. Patience is nothing other than self-control. Do not let internal enemies act as they would. Teach them to act *as you would have them*. Defeating them is akin to a valiant general crushing his foes.

To defeat external enemies, you must protect yourself *quickly* with the concept of respect.[12] For example, if you are ensconced in a castle with enemies on all four sides, you diligently protect yourself from the attackers and firmly defend the castle. You must take a similar approach with Nature's external forces. Do not use patience, but as the old saying goes, "Protect yourself from the wind as you would protect yourself from arrows." Respect the strength of your enemy, take cover, fortify your defenses, and guard your flank. Among the four elements, wind and cold are the ones for which you should have the most respect. It is not good to be exposed to the wind or cold for a long time.

For soundly defeating internal enemies, use courage.

For protecting yourself from external enemies, engage respect and beat a quick retreat.

24

Generally speaking, there are THREE PLEASURES OF HUMAN BEINGS. The first pleasure includes putting the Way[13] into practice, not being mistaken in yourself, and taking pleasure in the good. The second pleasure comes from enjoying a body free from illness, and in feeling happy. The third pleasure is in enjoying a long life.

You must develop a strategy for acquiring the three pleasures. If you do not acquire them, even if you are extraordinarily wealthy and respected, all will be for naught.

25

According to the reckoning of Shao Yao-fu,[14] Heaven and Earth have a fixed age of 129,600 years, and we are currently over halfway through this period.[15] Man is the spirit[16] of the Ten Thousand Things in Heaven and Earth, but his life does not extend beyond a hundred years. Heaven, Earth, and Man are called the Three Powers, but when we compare Man's life to that of Heaven and of Earth, our tears flow.

With a relatively short life, what kind of behavior is it *not* to practice the Way of Nurturing Life and, thus, to shorten the life Heaven has given you? Your life is extremely important. Do not turn your back on the Way.

26

The Way of Nurturing Life calls for you to exert yourself. As mentioned previously, you should move your body and circulate your *ch'i*. It is extremely harmful to embrace sleep, rest your body excessively, and develop habits of laziness. You should also limit your inaction. When you are stationary for a long time, your fundamental *ch'i* will not circulate, your respiration will stagnate, and you will become ill.

To exert your strength in serving your father and mother, to strive to serve your lord with sincerity and faithfulness, you must rise early in the morning, go to bed late at night, and exert yourself thoroughly in your own matters and chores, as do the four classes of people.[17]

From the time he is a child, a member of the warrior class reads books, practices calligraphy, studies etiquette and music, practices archery and horsemanship, and studies martial arts. He moves his body in every way. Likewise, from morning to night the farmers, artisans, and merchants exert themselves in their professions.

Women remain inside the house where it is easy for *ch'i* to stagnate and where they can easily get sick, so it is good for them to put themselves into their work and move their bodies. Even a young woman belonging to a wealthy and highly respected family works hard to serve her parents, parents-in-law, and husband. She weaves, sews, spins, prepares food, and brings up the children. Thus, she does not sit still for long. Amaterasu-o-mikami[18] wove the clothing of the gods herself. Her younger sister wove the clothing of the gods when she was in the sacred weaving hall. Such things are written in the *Nihon Shoki*.[19]

The four classes of people working hard at their own employments fall within the Way of Nurturing Life.

To make no efforts in the affairs in which you should exert yourself, to sit idle for a long time in a pleasant posture, to want to lie down and sleep—all of these are greatly harmful to your health. When such practices become entrenched, illnesses are many and life is short. You should be vigilant in this regard.

27

Different people have different vocations. They polish a vocation and add technique to their Way. For all vocations there are techniques in which you should become well versed. If you do not master the techniques, you will be unable to perform the tasks at hand. Even among the most trivial and humble accomplishments, if you do not have a command of the techniques, you will be incapable of the task. For example, making straw raincoats and papering umbrellas are extremely easy and humble vocations, but even there, if you do not study the techniques, you will be unable to do the job.

How much more so, then, for the Way of Nurturing Life in the human body of Man, which is said to be one of the Three Powers, along with Heaven and Earth? In short, if you are intent on taking care of yourself and living a long life, you must learn the appropriate techniques.

The COMMON PRACTICE FOR LEARNING A TECHNIQUE, even for some trivial art, is to seek out a teacher without fail, receive the teacher's instructions, and learn the proper techniques. Even the extremely talented will learn nothing if they do not have access to the techniques, a teacher, and instruction.

The techniques for nurturing your health are a full-fledged Great Way, not some small art. If you do not study the techniques with resolution, you will not master that Way. If you are able to study under a person who knows the techniques, do not trade the opportunity for a thousand pieces of gold.

When I look back on my youth in my hometown, there were many people who did not know the Way of Nurturing Life. They led dissipated and therefore short lives. Moreover, many of the old folks in my village, not knowing the Way, were often sick and in distress. Their health declined and they became doting old fools early on. In such cases, even if they lived to a hundred, their lives were without pleasure and full of aches and pains. A long life ill conceived is of no use. You may think that simply living long is a good thing, but longevity alone is not something for which you should be congratulated.

28

There is a dissenting theory that goes as follows: The Way of Nurturing Life may be fine for old retired people or for the young who lead idle and leisurely lives, but those with busy and active lives have no time to take care of their health. Warriors, who diligently serve their lords and parents with loyalty and filial piety, as well as farmers, artisans, and merchants whose daily efforts are strenuous, simply have no spare time.

These ideas reflect the self-doubt of a person who does not understand the techniques.

I am not saying that techniques are good only for those with leisure time. I am saying that it is good to keep your mind at peace and your body active. If your body is idle, your fundamental *ch'i* will stagnate and you will become ill. However, flowing water does not stagnate and the hinge on a well-used door never rusts. In other words, what moves, lives long; what doesn't move has a short life.

For this reason, it is good that warriors, farmers, artisans, and merchants exert themselves in their labors. It is not good to be idle. Their work flows naturally into the Way of Nurturing Life.

29

There is yet another doubt, which goes as follows: A person who follows the Way of Nurturing Life places importance only on his physical body and thinks that all is well as long as he preserves his life. The true gentleman,[20] however, values righteousness and will not regret losing his life. He will not think twice about danger or sacrificing his own life in the name of a righteous cause. He will face dangers outright and will die for the sake of principle. If he places too much importance on his body and acts so as not to harm the tiniest hair on his head, he will value his life over all else even when it comes to important matters and lose all sense of principle.

I would respond like this: generally speaking, events fall into two categories, the usual and the unusual. During the usual course of things, you behave as usual, but when the unusual arises, you should put the unusual into play.

It is good to act with righteousness at every moment. But in uneventful times, taking care of your body and following the Way of Nurturing Life corresponds to the usual. To give up your life without hesitation for a righteous cause corresponds to the unusual. If you are able to distinguish between usual and unusual events, doubts will not arise.

The Way of the Gentleman is correct when it is in accord with the moment. For example, in summer we wear a single layer of clothing, while in winter we wear several layers. Different events or circumstances quite naturally call for different actions.

If you do not follow the Way of Nurturing Life beforehand to increase your stamina, when some great event *does* happen and you must fight stubbornly, your body will be weak and you will be unable to accomplish your goal, whether or not you are forced to sacrifice your life. However, if you work to thoroughly nurture your *ch'i* during usual times, you will be able to summon your courage when the unusual occurs.

30

The men of long ago advocated self-control for the three desires of food/drink, sex, and sleep. People know that they should be careful about food, drink, and sex, but many are *unaware* that controlling your desire for sleep is also included in the Way of Nurturing Life.

You avoid illness when you reduce the hours you sleep because your fundamental *ch'i* can circulate more easily. When you oversleep, your fundamental *ch'i* does not circulate and you become ill. It is better to go to bed later at night. Sleeping during the day is the most harmful. Sleeping soon after sunset will block your respiration and cause harm. Most of all, whether morning or night, lying down quickly before your meal has been digested and your *ch'i* is not yet circulating, blocks your circulation and damages your fundamental health.

If you get into the habit of being lazy and dozing off, your sleeping will increase and you will be unable to control it. This parallels the temptations to overindulge in food, drink, and sex. You must control them resolutely in order to keep them in check. Make an effort to decrease the number of hours you sleep; when you become accustomed to this, you will naturally sleep less. The habit of sleeping less is something to which you should apply yourself.

31

You should also be circumspect in your speech, cut down on useless conversation, and become a person of few words. When you talk a lot, your *ch'i* will inevitably decrease. Being circumspect in your speech is the Way to nurture both your virtue and your body.

32

There is an old saying that goes, "Colossal misfortunes occur from being unable to endure the moment." In other words, in a short period of time, huge disasters can occur.

There are cases of people becoming ill because they were unable to control themselves over a cupful of wine[21] and half a bowl of food. They indulged their desire a little more, but the harm they incurred was great. If a flame the size of a firefly's illumination ignites a house, it will lead to a great disaster. An old saying has it that "The moment the crime was committed was as insignificant as an autumn hair,[22] but the disease that was contracted [in that moment] was as heavy as Mt. T'ai." This is truly well said.

Generally speaking, there are any number of small affairs that turn into great misfortunes. In regard to contracting a disease, a small mistake can turn into a great tragedy. You must be vigilant concerning things of this sort. You should take these two ancient sayings to heart and not forget them.

33

There are many people who are young, healthy, and strong by birth, but are unable to fulfill the years allotted to them and die young because they do not follow the Way of Nurturing Life. This is not a disaster dropped on them from Heaven, but one they bring on themselves. Nor can we pass off their early death by saying they have lived their allotted time.

A strong man who has confidence in his own strength may be careless and die earlier than a weak man. By contrast, there are any number of people with weak constitutions who lack proper food and drink, are constantly sick, and suppose that they will die young. Yet, such people may live long lives because they stand in respect of their own weakness and are exceedingly careful.

Therefore, whether you have the potential for a long or short life is not contingent upon your being strong or weak. It is a matter of whether or not you take care of your life. Po Chu-i[23] said, "Good fortune and disaster depend on being or not being circumspect." The same applies to long life.

34

In our world many people are terribly concerned about acquiring property, social status, and income; and though they flatter others and pray to the gods and buddhas, it all comes to naught. Very few people seek a Way to live a long life, maintain their health, and be free from disease.

Property, social status, and revenue are external matters. Living a long life and being disease-free are internal matters. When we seek the former and ignore the latter, we are liable to find the former just as the latter expires.

A long life and freedom from illness are easily attained if you seek them. What sort of matter is it to search for the difficult but not for the easily gained? It is absolutely foolish. Even if you manage to obtain property and income, if you are always sick and have a short life, it comes to nothing.

35

The *ch'i* of yin and yang exists in the firmament; it flows along as a current and does not stagnate. For this reason, spring, summer, fall, and winter move along smoothly, and the generation of the Ten Thousand Things in Heaven and Earth continues successfully. If the *ch'i* of yin and yang becomes distorted and stagnates, the path of its flow is obstructed. Then, winters are hot, summers are cold, and there are strange changes in the weather such as torrential rains, strong winds, and bad harvests. Calamities occur.

This pattern holds true for the human body as well. If your *ch'i* and blood circulate well and do not stagnate, your *ch'i* will be strong and you will not become ill. However, if your *ch'i* and blood do not circulate, you will get sick. If your *ch'i* stagnates in your upper body, you will suffer headaches and dizziness; if it stagnates in the middle, you will have pains in your heart and stomach; if it stagnates in your lower body, you may suffer lumbago, beriberi, painful urination, and hemorrhoids.

For this reason, people who apply the principles of the Way of Nurturing Life do their best to keep their fundamental *ch'i* from stagnating.

36

People who aspire to following the Way of Nurturing Life must always have the master in their hearts.[24] When the master is there, you consider things deeply: you distinguish right from wrong, suppress your anger, and keep your desires in check, and so your mistakes are few. When the master is absent, you are careless in thought, you are unable to control your desires and anger, you do as you please regardless of the consequences, and you make many mistakes.

37

In almost any situation, giving in to a momentary impulse is likely to lead to disaster at a later date. Consuming all the wine and food you desire feels good at the time, but if you continue down such a path you're likely to become ill. If you practice self-control from the outset, you will no doubt rejoice later on, just as enduring the heat of moxa cautery for a short period of time yields benefits in improved health afterward. There is a line in one of Tu Mu's[25] poems that goes, "You persevere, then bear it with pleasure." This alludes to the idea of controlling temptation until it passes, thereby harvesting the long-term benefits and the feelings of pleasure that come from being in a good situation.

38

The saying "The sage treats the not-yet-ill" means that if you are careful beforehand, you will avoid illness altogether. This is great good fortune.

Sun Tzu[26] said, "The man who uses his army well performs no outstanding meritorious deeds." In other words, the man who skillfully puts his army's resources in play appears, from the outside, to be doing very little at all. Why? Because he defeats the enemy before the battle ever begins. Sun Tzu further said, "The ancients who were skillful at defeating the enemy were those who defeated the easily defeated."

You must do the same with the Way of Nurturing Life. You must single-mindedly commit yourself to being victorious *before* the battle (the onset of illness) occurs. Like a talented general, you conquer easily defeated foes, such as desires and temptations, and thus do not become ill at all. This is the best strategy. This is the strategy of healing the not-yet-ill.

39

The Way of Nurturing Life requires that you *not* give in to selfish impulses. It requires intense circumspection. When you follow your temptations you are being selfish. When you practice respect,[27] you are practicing circumspection. Follow the common maxim: "In being careful, be a coward."

Sun Chen-jen[28] said that "Nurturing health has its foundation in respect." There is no place for gallantry in the Way of Nurturing Life. Be respectful and circumspect, as you would when crossing a bridge made of very small logs.

40

To maintain your health, you must rely on the Way of Nurturing Life. You cannot put your trust in acupuncture, moxa cautery, or medicine.

In the teachings of the ancients can be found the highest laws for nurturing your health. Mencius himself called for "decreasing desires." The Sung-dynasty scholar Wang Chao-su also declared that "There is nothing better for nurturing your body than cutting down on your desires." And in the *Sheng Hsin Lu*, it states that "When your desires are many, your life will be worn out."

The educated warrior should always consider this instruction.

41

Ch'i must be made to permeate your entire body. It is wrong to allow it to collect in one place in your chest. When anger, sorrow, anxiety, and yearning arise, *ch'i* will gather and stagnate in one place in your chest. When you are excessive with your seven emotions, your *ch'i* will stagnate and you will become ill.

42

The common person gives in to his desires and turns his back on societal courtesy; he does not nurture his *ch'i* and, therefore, does not maintain the longevity given to him by Heaven. Thus, he loses both principle and *ch'i*.

The cultured warrior who knows the techniques of the mountain hermits single-mindedly devotes himself to nurturing his *ch'i*, loves the principles of the Way, but tosses aside societal courtesy.

The stubborn Confucianist is obstinate, concentrating on manners and rites, and does not nourish his *ch'i*. Ignorant of the Way of self-cultivation and training, he does not live out his given years.

None of these three understands the Way in which the true gentleman acts.

Good Habits, Bad Habits

43

Generally speaking, you should rise early, wash your hands and face, arrange your hair, and do the morning's chores.

After eating, you should rub your abdomen in a downward motion a number of times to stimulate your breathing. It is also good to rub the area on the left side of your belly in a diagonal motion with the inside of your index finger a number of times. In addition, you should rub your hips in a downward motion and gently strike the lower parts. You should not strike them forcefully. If your breathing is obstructed, look up and breathe out any noxious air three or four times.

After morning and evening meals, you should move about. You

should not sit for a long time and you should never lie down or sleep. This lack of activity will obstruct your *ch'i*, make you ill, and, if it becomes habitual, can shorten your life. It is always good to walk about three hundred paces after eating. From time to time, a walk of six to seven hundred yards would be even better.

44

If you are at home, it is good to do some light exercise from time to time. Activity such as standing up and sitting down should be considered beneficial, not troublesome. Servants should not do so much that you become inactive. You should handle some of the chores in your room; things get done more quickly and better when you do them yourself, so don't bother with servants. This is the advantage of "cleansing your mind and reducing your affairs." When you are constantly moving your body in this way, your *ch'i* and blood will circulate well and your breathing will not be sluggish.

This is an essential method for the Way of Nurturing Life.

Avoid idleness. When you set yourself up with a reasonable number of things to do, you put your hands and feet to work. Then your *ch'i* will circulate, not stagnate. Be careful not to tire yourself out. It is advisable to be neither too stationary nor too mobile.

45

Among the sayings of Doctor Hua T'o[29] is the following: "The body should labor. If it does, the vitality of the grain [one eats] will dissolve, and blood will circulate freely throughout the vascular system."

Generally speaking, if you reduce your physical desires, exercise from time to time, put your hands and feet to work, walk and do not sit in one place for too long, your *ch'i* and blood should circulate well and not stagnate. This is important business for the Way of Nurturing Life, and you must do it daily.

In the *Lu Shih Ch'un Ch'iu*,[30] it says, "Flowing water does not stagnate, the busy door pivot does not become worm-eaten. This is because they move. Form and *ch'i* are both naturally so." Stationary water, an unused door—both will deteriorate if not put to use. When in motion, no disaster befalls them.

Your body is exactly the same.

46

In the Way of Nurturing Life in the *Ch'ien Chin Fang*,[31] it declares that you should not "be active for a long time, sit for a long time, lie down for a long time, or look fixedly at something for a long time."

47

When you lie down and sleep before the *ch'i* of your wine and food has been digested, the wine and food will assuredly be delayed in their passage. Never lie down during the day; doing so will cause great damage to your fundamental health.

The exception is when you are severely exhausted. If this is the case, it is fine to lean your back against something and sleep. But if you lie down, sleep for a short while. To avoid oversleeping, have someone awaken you at a predetermined time.

48

Even in the summer when the days are long, you should not lie down during the day. Some people are exhausted by evening and quickly go to sleep. In order to avoid this temptation, you should move about after your evening meal. Take a walk. After the sun sets, it is acceptable to lie down to give your body and *ch'i* some rest. But it is *not* acceptable to go to sleep. Sleeping at this time can be extraordinarily injurious. Moreover, you should not lie down for long; once the lamps are lit, you should get up into a sitting position.

If you follow this practice, you will have physical strength and will not quickly become sleepy. The best course of action is to avoid lying down soon after sunset.

49

In the Way of Nurturing Life, too much self-confidence is taboo. To be overly confident in your own strength or youth, or to take illness lightly, are the foundations of unhappiness. For example, if you are overconfident in the ability of your blade to cut well, your blade may break when you put it to use. If you are overly confident in the strength of your own *ch'i* and put unreasonable demands on it, your *ch'i* will lose its force. If you are overly confident in the strength of your spleen and kidneys and consume excessive amounts of food and drink or overindulge in sex, you will become ill.

50

If someone were to throw jewels at sparrows to scare them off, he would be declared a fool for giving up something so valuable to gain something so trivial. If you succumb to trivial desires at the expense of your body, it is exactly like throwing jewels at sparrows.

51

The mind must enjoy itself. It should not be in distress. The body must exert itself. It should not take too much rest. By eating too many savory foods, drinking too much delicious wine, taking too much pleasure in sex, offering too many pleasures to the body while embracing idleness and sleep, you will spoil yourself and your actions will lead—contrary to your intentions—to your physical deterioration.

Likewise, going to opposite extremes is of no use. To thoughtlessly drink large amounts of supplementary medicines[32] when you aren't sick is another form of spoiling yourself, and may lead to illness.

In the end, excessively spoiling the child leads to unhappiness.

52

Ruining the body you could use for a hundred years due to a lack of self-control is true foolishness. Controlling your desires is the foundation of living a long and pleasant life. Overindulging your desires is the foundation for shortening your life.

Controlling or overindulging is the fork in the road along the Way of Nurturing Life.

53

In the *I Ching* it says, "Thoughts of anxiety—guard against these ahead of time." This means that if you think of the pain that will follow an action—that is, think of the consequences—you can prevent unhappiness. In the *Analects of Confucius* it says, "If a man does not think far ahead, surely there will be trouble close by."

Both of these phrases clearly tell us that if you practice caution at an early stage, you should be free from danger later on.

54

It is helpful to take a look around and compare how other people nurture their fundamental health on a daily basis, from morning to night, or how they damage their health with equal persistence.

There are many people who, in a single day, do not nurture their *ch'i* even a little, and many who damage it constantly. In the Way of Nurturing Life, you must make efforts solely to nurture your fundamental health, and take care never to cause it harm.

If you take a middle road and the damage exceeds the nurturing day in and day out over a long period of time, your fundamental health will diminish, you will become ill, and you could die.

This is, in fact, why many people become sick and die. They shorten their lives in minute increments.

There is a limit to your fundamental health, but your desires are without end.

To give in to those desires is disgraceful.

55

Among the sayings of the ancients there is this: "Throughout a single day, be circumspect of that day alone. In this way, your life will be long, and in the end you will suffer no disasters."

The meaning is clear: If you examine yourself one day at a time and every day exhibit common sense from morning to night, you will make no mistakes regarding your constitution, you will not damage your health, you will live a long time, and you will suffer no disasters for your allotted span of life.

This is an essential method of preserving your health.

56

It is not necessary to say a lot about the Way of Nurturing Life. Just be sparing with your food and drink, do not eat things that will promote illness, be circumspect about sexual desire, do not waste your pure *ch'i*,[33] and do not be excessive with anger, grief, anxiety, or longing. Put your mind at peace and your *ch'i* in harmony, use few words, and reduce unnecessary affairs. Protect yourself against the negative external influences of wind, cold, heat, and humidity. Move your body from time to time, take walks, do not sleep when it is not time to do so, and keep your respiration circulating well. These are the ESSENTIAL POINTS OF THE WAY OF NURTURING LIFE AND HEALTH.

57

Food and drink nurture your body, while sleep nurtures your *ch'i*. However, going to excesses with food and drink will damage your spleen and stomach, while excessive sleeping when it is unnecessary will damage your fundamental health.

The health-conscious person rises early, goes to bed late, takes no midday naps, is never idle, and always makes great efforts in his duties. He reduces his hours of sleep, refreshes his spirit, decreases the amount of his food and drink, and keeps his mind clean.[34]

Living like this, your fundamental health will be hearty, your circulation will not be hindered, the *ch'i* that you were born with will receive its due of nourishment, your vigor will flourish on its own, and you will not become ill.

The appropriate regulation of food and sleep are also ESSENTIAL POINTS OF THE WAY OF NURTURING LIFE AND HEALTH.

58

If the poor take pleasure in the Way of Nurturing Life every day, then they, too, can live happy lives. When they enjoy the benefits of good health, the hours of each passing day will be long and filled with pleasure. And within the passing of a single year, such people will daily take the highest joy in such simple pleasures as the changing seasons. How great will their pleasures be!

Thus, many years will pass, the pleasures of those years will be prolonged, and the effects of those pleasures should be manifested as longevity.

Even if it is difficult for us to obtain the heights of pleasure enjoyed by a sage or a man of great humanity, we can come close to their levels, benefiting from a long life and the resultant feelings of happiness.

59

Putting your mind at peace, making your *ch'i* harmonious, keeping your words few, and speaking in a calm manner—this is NURTURING YOUR VIRTUE *and* nurturing your health.

For these things, the Way is the same. When your words are many, your mind becomes excited and your *ch'i* becomes rough. This damages your virtue and damages your health. For these things, the injuries are the same.

60

Of the people who live in the mountains, there are many who are long lived. In one of the ancient writings, it says, "In the atmosphere of the mountains, there is much longevity." And, "In a cold atmosphere, there is longevity."

In a cold climate, the fundamental *ch'i* of the body is sealed. It is preserved inside and does not escape. For this reason, one's life is long. In warm climates, the fundamental *ch'i* escapes, is less likely to be preserved within, and life is short.

Moreover, people in the mountains have fewer social associations and so are at peace. With peace, their fundamental health does not diminish. Further, as they have fewer material goods and conveniences, they have fewer desires. A wide variety of delicious fish is particularly lacking, and they can never eat a bellyful of meat. These are reasons people in the mountains are long lived.

In the cities, a man's social associations are numerous and his chores various and many, so his *ch'i* decreases. People who live by the sea always eat a surfeit of fish and meat. Feasting to their heart's content, they become ill and their life is shortened.

But even if you choose to live in a city or close to the sea, if your desires are few and you eat less meat, you should suffer no damage.

61

To live alone, to pass the day in peace, to read old books and recite the poetry of the ancients; to light incense, to amuse yourself with folding books containing copies of ancient calligraphy; to gaze at the mountains and rivers, to look appreciatively at the moon and flowers, to love the grasses and trees and enjoy the passing of the four seasons; to drink wine until pleasantly drunk and adorn your plate with vegetables from your own garden—these are all methods of pleasing your mind and NURTURING YOUR *CH'I*.

The poor, too, can obtain these pleasures at any time; if they understand them well, they are better off than being rich and not understanding them at all.

62

An ancient saying has it that "Patience[35] is the jewel of the body." If you can be patient, you will not be unhappy; if you cannot be patient, you will be unhappy. Patience is a matter of self-control. It is putting a limit on desires. You must be patient with both anger and desire, because in large part, the Way of Nurturing Life is in self-control over these emotions. Therefore, you should observe this one word: patience.

Among Wu Wang's[36] precepts is this: "If you can be patient with something for just a moment, you will make your body replete." In the *Shang Shu*[37] it says, "If you have patience, you are certain to have results." Another saying of the ancients has it that "Great disasters occur from a moment's lack of patience."

Thus we say that this one word—patience—is the Way of nurturing both your health and your virtue.

63

The CH'I OF THE STOMACH[38] is another name for fundamental health. This is a *ch'i* of *tranquility and harmony*. Even if he has a grave illness, a person with this *ch'i* will live. A person without this *ch'i* will die.

The pulse[39] of the *ch'i* of the stomach is not long, short, slow, fast, great, or small, but is exactly fitting to a person's age, more or less pliant, and balanced. You cannot give a name to this pulse. You can only perceive it yourself. The pulse of a person whose fundamental health has not declined and who is without disease is like this. This is a teaching of the ancients. A person who is following the Way of Nurturing Life should always seek to have such a pulse.

A person who is neglecting his health and whose *ch'i* has diminished will have a weak pulse here even though he is young. This is a sick person. A person with a weak pulse and no *ch'i* of the stomach will die.

Moreover, a person with spirit in his eyes will live long. A person without that spirit will have a short life. When you examine a person who is ill, you should consider this fact.

64

The Way of Nurturing Life should be practiced in the same manner Chuang Tzu[40] recommended using a butcher's knife to cut up an ox: follow the natural flow.

There is a space between the joints of an ox's bones, and the blade of the knife is thin. If you take that thin blade and move it through the wide space between the bones of the joints, there will be plenty of room for the blade to do its work without being impeded by the bones. In this way, Chuang Tzu's butcher cut up oxen for nineteen years without once sharpening his blade.

Though you live in the world, you broaden your mind and do not fight with things; if you conduct yourself according to principle,[41] you will not be impeded by the world, and Heaven and Earth themselves will be broad.

A person who acts in this manner will have a long life.

65

If your joy or pleasure with other people is too extreme, your *ch'i* will be open to excess and diminish. When you are alone and experience too much anxiety and grief, your *ch'i* will be bound up and obstructed. To be either diminished or obstructed harms your fundamental health.

66

Here is the WAY OF NURTURING YOUR MIND AND YOUR *CH'I*. The samurai who wishes to safeguard his health should follow this path:

+ Put your mind at peace and do not be flustered; be loose and anxiety free.
+ Make your *ch'i* gentle and unruffled; let your words be few, keep

your voice from growing shrill, and do not laugh too loud.

+ Bring joy to your heart, and be slow to anger.
+ Make your sorrows few, and do not lament over what cannot be changed.
+ If you make a mistake, bring yourself to account once, but do not grieve over that mistake a second time.
+ Be satisfied with Heaven's command,[42] and don't brood over your troubles.

67

Saliva is the moisture of the entire body. It changes and becomes pure blood. If grasses and trees do not have their own pure liquid, they will wither. Thus, it is very important.

Saliva comes to the mouth from the internal organs. Value it highly and do not just spit it out. You should especially not spit great distances, as this diminishes *ch'i*.

68

You should swallow your saliva; do not spit it out. Phlegm, however, you should expectorate; do *not* swallow it.

Dispose of phlegm from your mouth or throat on a sheet of paper; do not spit it out at a distance. If saliva or water coagulates and becomes phlegm, that phlegm will not become saliva, so you should expectorate it. Phlegm obstructs your *ch'i* and causes harm. Swallowing phlegm instead of expelling it is a mistake.

When you spit out phlegm, you must not disperse *ch'i*.

When you drink a lot of wine, it creates phlegm, causes your *ch'i* to increase, and reduces the amount of your saliva.

No matter what you do, if you hurry through it, even while trying to do it well, it will turn out poorly. If you select a treatment for an illness in haste or cast around for a physician at random, you are likely to pay dearly for this behavior.

The same holds true when choosing one of the various massage techniques or a hot springs cure. You must not arbitrarily choose a treatment. First determine what is appropriate. A haphazard selection could worsen your illness or even bring on death.

Generally speaking, use one or more of the six kinds of treatments—medicine, acupuncture, moxa, the two types of massage,[43] and hot springs—*after* you have clearly determined what is appropriate.

70

For the most part, both good and bad arise from habits. Being circumspect in taking care of your health and making an effort to support it will create good habits. If you avoid laziness, exert yourself in the field of health, and put into practice the Way of Nurturing Life and other tips on well being, you will become accustomed to following this path. The results will be beneficial and constant, and you will live without pain.

If you are not circumspect and create unhealthful and bad habits, when you *do* exert yourself to improve your health, it will be painful and hard to bear.

71

You must calculate your own strength in everything you do. To push matters beyond your own capacity will reduce your *ch'i* and bring on illness. You should not exert yourself beyond your own limits.

72

You must be careful about your fundamental health from the time you are young and healthy and throughout your old age. When you are young, you should not simply rely on your strength or overuse your fundamental health. To deal lightly with your fundamental health while you are young will lead to your decline as you grow old.

Taking care of your body only after it has grown weak is like squandering riches when you are wealthy and economizing only after you become poor. While this late effort is better than continuing on the same downward course, it will yield lesser results. Your life will be the poorer for it.

73

In nurturing your *ch'i*, you should use the word "sparing." Lao Tzu also speaks of this. To be sparing is to value something. When you value your fundamental health, you will not squander it. For example, a stingy man may have great wealth, but he will value it and not give it away. If you value your *ch'i*, your fundamental health will not decline and you will live a long time.

74

The essentials of nurturing your health lie in avoiding self-deception and in being patient. Self-deception is a matter of being amenable to doing something even though you know in your heart that it is wrong. For example, although you know that overeating is bad for you, you will still indulge if you do not truly abhor it. You should be able to understand everything else from this example.

When you look at the people around you, the majority of them appear to have been given long lives. But being ignorant of the techniques of the Way of Nurturing Life, they do not put the techniques into practice and so do not maintain the potential for longevity with which they were born.

Let's take the case of P'eng Tzu.[44] If he had taken a knife and cut his own throat, would he not have died rather than live as long as he did? When people today damage their lives by letting their desires run rampant, they are cutting their own throats. Theirs may be a slow deterioration rather than a quick death, but it is death by their own hand nonetheless.

A person with strong *ch'i* who should live for a long time will surely shorten his life by not nurturing that *ch'i*.

If you seek to have everything perfect around you, your mind will be filled with anxiety and you will find little pleasure in life. Disasters occur from this attitude. Moreover, if you want other people to be perfect according to your own definition of perfection, you will fixate on their insufficiencies with indignation and this will give your mind further worries.

You should not take pleasure in the absolute perfection of your everyday food and drink, clothing, utensils, household, and plants. Rather, if they are just a little pleasing, this should be sufficient. Do not seek or await perfect beauty; find a little pleasure in what is already there. This is another means of nurturing your *ch'i*.

A certain person said, "We all know that being circumspect with our desires for food, drink, and sex is the Way of Nurturing Life. But being circumspect is difficult, while doing what we please is easy. So nurturing our health is troublesome."

I think he says this because he *still* does not understand the techniques of nurturing health. If he *did* understand them, how could he *not* put them into practice?

If you submerge yourself in water, you will flounder and drown. If you walk into a fire, you will burn and die. If you eat arsenic, you will be poisoned and die. Everybody knows these things, so no one submerges himself in water, walks into a fire, or eats arsenic. If you *know* that ruining your life with many desires and that cutting your throat with a knife amount to the same thing in the end, why aren't you patient with your desires?

Because people become confused, make mistakes, and encounter disaster out of ignorance. It is the same with the infant who crawls up to a well, falls in, and dies: he was ignorant of the danger.

If you show no humanity and bring people to pain and suffering, you will suffer Heaven's retribution, be blamed by others, and surely bring disaster upon yourself as well. Yet, while this principle is perfectly clear, fools are ignorant of it.

When you have knowledge you benefit. Because you know that by using moxa you will eliminate your disease, you do not mind applying the fire to your body and bearing the heat and pain a number of times. You bear the burden for the benefit.

If you clearly understand the techniques for the Way of Nurturing Life, why would you simply follow your desires without any circumspection?

78

Sages are inclined to expound on pleasure. And while our own foolishness makes it difficult to gauge a sage's mind, pleasure is found in the life principle of Heaven and Earth, which is ours at birth. You must not turn away from the principle of Heaven and Earth, but neither must you relinquish your right to take pleasure in things.

By means of the Way, you can regulate your desires, avoid overindulgence, and not be deprived of pleasure.

79

The TECHNIQUE FOR ATTAINING LONGEVITY lies in decreasing your desires for food and sex, pacifying your mind and *ch'i*, and looking at things carefully and always deporting yourself with respect[45] and circumspection. If you do this, you will not be frustrated by the things you encounter, your blood and *ch'i* will become regulated by themselves, and you will naturally have no illnesses.

This is the technique for longevity. If you follow these guidelines, you will live a long time. If you have faith in this technique and put it into practice, you will find its value to be much greater than ten thousand pieces of gold.

80

In all things, when they are replete to the point where nothing could be added, they will have become the foundation of sorrow. The ancients said, "Drink wine until you're lightly drunk; view the cherry blossoms when they are only half open." These are excellent words to be sure.

When you drink as much wine as you can hold, you will suffer damage. When you drink just a little, short of satiety, you will feel pleasure but no distress afterward. When cherry blossoms are in full bloom, they will have gone beyond their peak, lost their spirit, and be quick to fall. The ancients also said that cherry blossoms have reached their peak before they have bloomed.

81

The Way of Nurturing Life is in observing the mean. Observing the mean has been defined as "neither going too far nor stopping too short." When food has relieved your hunger, you should stop eating. This is observing the mean.

All things should be just like this.

82

Your mind should always be composed, quiet, and without any sort of restlessness. It should be at peace. Your words, especially, should be calm and few in number. You should not talk about things of no use. This is, indeed, an excellent method of nurturing your *ch'i*.

83

The human body has its fount of life in *ch'i*, and *ch'i* is the master of one's fate. Thus, the person who cares for it well will always value his fundamental health and act so as not to diminish it.

When at peace, you preserve your fundamental health; when in motion, you circulate it. Preservation and circulation—if you are not possessed of these two, it will be difficult to nurture your *ch'i*.

Do not miss the moments for preservation and circulation; this is the Way of Nurturing *Ch'i*.

When there are strong winds, violent rains, or thunder, you should have respect for the majesty of Heaven. And, though it may be the dead of night, you should always get up, change your clothes, and sit. You should not lie down.

When you are a guest at another's residence during the day, you should return home before nightfall. If you continue talking into the night, both host and guest will become tired. You should not remain seated for long periods of time.

In *The Yellow Emperor's Classic on Medicine*,[46] it says, "When angry, your *ch'i* inflates; when rejoicing, your *ch'i* is not stable. When sad, your *ch'i* dies out; when frightened, your *ch'i* does not circulate. When cold, your *ch'i* closes up; when hot, your *ch'i* leaks away. When alarmed, your *ch'i* is in confusion; when tired, your *ch'i* decreases. When sunk deep in thought, your *ch'i* becomes knotted."

The hundred diseases are all associated with *ch'i*. Disease results when *ch'i* is afflicted.[47] Thus, the Way of Nurturing Life lies in regulating your *ch'i*. The regulation of your *ch'i* lies in its harmonization and pacification.

Generally, the Way of Nurturing *Ch'i* is in neither decreasing nor obstructing it. If you harmonize and pacify your *ch'i*, you should have no worries.

The *tan t'ien*[48] is situated three *tsun*[49] below your navel. The *ch'i* that moves between the two kidneys is located here. In the *Nan Ching*[50] it says, "The moving *ch'i* between the kidneys and below the navel is the very life of the human being. It is the foundation of the Twelve Meridians."[51] This is the place that is the foundation of life for the human being's body.

For the TECHNIQUE OF NURTURING YOUR CH'I, you should always sit[52] with your hips[53] in the proper position, bring your pure *ch'i* into your *tan t'ien*, breathe peacefully without letting your breath become rough and, as you become calm, bring the *ch'i* from your chest lightly[54] and repeatedly disgorge it into your mouth. You should *not* collect *ch'i* in your chest but, rather, should collect it in the *tan t'ien*. Thus, your *ch'i* will not rise, your chest will not become agitated, and your body will have force. You should also do this when you are speaking to a member of the nobility, or when you are facing some great emergency and are hurried. When you have to argue with someone out of sheer necessity, this practice will not fail you in preventing you from acting carelessly or being offended by the other person's anger.

When you make efforts in the various arts and their specific techniques, or when as a warrior you grasp the sword or spear and confront the enemy, you should consider this to be your principal method of preparation. If you exert yourself in this technique, it will be of great benefit in nurturing your *ch'i*.

Anyone who practices a technique, but especially warriors, must understand this method. The method of bringing the essence of *ch'i* below the navel is also appropriate for Taoists nurturing their *ch'i* and monks practicing zazen.

This is a practice that will bring you peace.

It is also the secret key to the arts.

88

The SEVEN EMOTIONS are joy, anger, depression, pleasure, love, hate, and desire. In the medical profession we consider them to be joy, anger, anxiety, yearning, sorrow, fear, and astonishment. There are, moreover, SIX DESIRES, which are those of the ear, eye, mouth, nose, body, and mind.

Of the seven emotions, anger and desire most seriously break down your virtue and damage your life. The *I Ching* admonishes us to "suppress anger and choke off desires."

Anger belongs to yang. It is similar to the burning action of fire. Anger confuses the mind of man and damages his fundamental health. It should be controlled with patience. Desire belongs to yin. It works like deep water. Desire drowns the mind of man and reduces his fundamental health.

You should think this over and choke off these two emotions.

89

There is a secret key to nurturing your health. This key is an essential secret transmission that any person aiming to take good care of himself must understand and observe. The secret key is in the single word *decrease*.[55] Decrease means to reduce all of your ten thousand affairs and avoid increasing them. Be frugal in everything or, in other words, decrease your desires.

Your desires are said to be the greed and fondnesses of the ear, eye, mouth, and body. They are variations of the fondness for wine, food, and sex. Generally speaking, accumulated desires damage the body and result in a loss of life. If you can decrease your desires, you will nourish your body and extend the years of your life.

In decreasing your desires, there is a list of twelve items. We call them the TWELVE REDUCTIONS,[56] which you should observe with consistency. They are as follows:

- decrease your food
- decrease your drink
- decrease your propensity for the "five tastes"
- decrease your desire for sex
- decrease your volume of words
- decrease your affairs
- decrease your anger
- decrease your anxieties
- decrease your sorrows
- decrease your yearning
- decrease your hours of sleep

If you can decrease each and every one of these, your fundamental health will not be reduced and your kidneys and spleen will not suffer damage. Indeed, this is the Way of maintaining your longevity.

But this key is not limited to twelve items. You should decrease your desires in general and use this key as a guideline for everything you do.

If you should at once overuse your *ch'i* or your mind, your fundamental health will be reduced, you will become ill, and you will shorten your life.

Your various affairs should not be many in number or wide in breadth. It is better for them to be fewer in number and narrower in breadth.

Sun Chen-mo also mentions the Twelve Reductions in the *Ch'ien Ssu Fang*.[57] His intention is the same, although his list is different. The above twelve practices are in accord with the times.

90

Reducing your internal desires, fending off the negative external influences, exerting yourself from time to time, and decreasing the number of hours of sleep: these four are the Great Essentials of the Way of Nurturing Life.

91

You must pacify your *ch'i* and not allow it to be rough in any way. *Ch'i* should be tranquil; it should not be moved chaotically. It should move gently and slowly, in an unhurried manner. You should speak with few words and not move your *ch'i* when speaking. You should always collect your *ch'i* beneath your navel and not allow it to rise to your chest. These are methods of nurturing your *ch'i*.

92

The ancients chanted poems and danced, and thus nurtured their blood vessels.[58] Chanting poems means singing; dancing means moving the hands and stamping the feet. Both of these pacify the mind, move the body, circulate the *ch'i*, and nurture the body. They circulate the *ch'i* much as the two kinds of massage do today.[59]

93

For nurturing yourself, follow the FOUR REDUCTIONS:

+ To nurture your spirit,[60] reduce your worries.
+ To nurture your essence, reduce your desires.
+ To nurture your stomach, reduce your food and drink.
+ To nurture your *ch'i*, reduce your words.

94

In taking care of yourself, there are SEVEN WAYS OF NURTURING YOUR HEALTH, and you should observe them all. First, by decreasing your words, you nurture your inner *ch'i*; second, by being cautious about sexual desire, you nurture your essential *ch'i*[61]; third, by decreasing your penchant for delicious foods, you nourish your vigor; fourth, by swallowing your saliva, you nourish the *ch'i* of your inner organs; fifth, by controlling your anger, you nourish the *ch'i* of your liver; sixth, by being temperate with your food and drink, you nourish the *ch'i* of your stomach; and seventh, by decreasing your worries, you nourish the *ch'i* of your mind.

These all appear in the *Shou Ch'in Yang Lao Shu*.[62]

95

Sun Chen-mo said, "In self-cultivation, there are the Five Goods. It is good to keep your hair well trimmed; it is good to have your hands on your face; it is good to lightly clack your teeth together a number of times, as though you were eating something; it is good to swallow your saliva; and it is always good to train your *ch'i*." To "train your *ch'i*" means to "pacify it and to keep it from becoming turbulent."

96

You should not walk for a long time, stand for a long time, talk for a long time, sit for a long time, or lie down for a long time. To expend a great deal of energy for a long time, reduces your *ch'i*. To be at rest for a long time obstructs *ch'i*. Reducing and obstructing *ch'i* both damage the body.

97

The FOUR ESSENTIALS for nurturing your health are avoiding violent anger, reducing your worries, reducing the number of your words, and reducing your appetites.

98

In the *Ping Yuan Chi*, Doctor T'ang Ch'un[63] says, "The Four Injuries are these: spitting a long distance injures *ch'i*, sleeping for a long time injures the spirit, sweating a lot injures the blood, and walking too quickly injures the tendons."

99

Old folks should not use strong medicines for ridding themselves of phlegm. If they try to rid themselves entirely of phlegm, their *ch'i* will decrease. This is a teaching of the ancients.

100

The breath always leaves and enters the body through the nose. Exhaling expels the interior *ch'i*. Inhaling draws in exterior *ch'i*. Respiration is the life[64] of man. If there is no respiration, he dies.

The *ch'i* inside man is the same as the *ch'i* of the universe. It passes back and forth between interior and exterior. Man exists in the midst of this UNIVERSAL CH'I just as a fish exists in the midst of water. The water inside the fish is the water outside of it, passing in and out. In the same way, the *ch'i* inside man is the same *ch'i* as that of the universe. The *ch'i* inside man, however, has passed through his organs and viscera and has thus aged and become polluted. The universal *ch'i* is always new and pure.

From time to time you should draw in a good quantity of this exterior *ch'i* through your nose. When much of the *ch'i* you have drawn in has collected inside you, it should be quietly expelled, little by little, through your mouth. You should not expel it quickly or roughly. After expelling the old and polluted *ch'i*, you draw in the new, pure *ch'i*. This is an exchange of the old and the new.

When you do this, your posture should be correct. You should look upward, stretch out your legs, close your eyes, and draw your hands into tight fists. The distance between your feet should be five *tsun*, and your elbows should each be about five *tsun* from your body. You should practice this once or twice between morning and night. If you do so over a period of time, you will see results. You should practice this only after having pacified your *ch'i*.

101

In the *Ch'ien Chin Fang* we are instructed to always draw in pure *ch'i* through the nose and to expel impure *ch'i* through the mouth. Draw in a large quantity, but expel just a little. In exhalation, the mouth is opened to make a thin aperture, and the *ch'i* is expelled only bit by bit.

102

Breath should always be slow and drawn deeply into the *tan t'ien*. This should not be done quickly.

103

The METHOD OF METERED BREATHING consists of regulating your respiration, making it tranquil, and expelling the breath in small amounts, little by little. If you continue in this practice for some time, you will eventually feel as though no breath is passing through your nose at all. You will simply feel the coming and going of small amounts of breath from above the navel. Practicing in this way, your energy will become regulated.

This is a technique for nurturing your *ch'i*. Respiration is the thoroughfare for *ch'i* entering and exiting your body. This should not be done roughly.

104

It will be difficult to put the techniques of the Way of Nurturing Life into practice if you are not first circumspect and carefully observant of the LAWS OF THE MIND. The mind must be made peaceful and free from agitation. Anger should be controlled and desires decreased. You should always enjoy yourself and be free from anxiety.

If you do not observe the laws of the mind, the Way of Nurturing Life cannot be put into practice. Thus, nurturing the mind and nurturing the body are not separate; they are a single endeavor.

105

Reading books and having conversations with others at night should not go beyond the beginning of the third watch. The night is divided into five watches,[65] so the third watch is halfway between the fourth and the ninth temple bells that notify the public of the time. If you do not go to sleep by midnight, your spirit will not become calm.

106

If the exterior environment is clean and pure, the interior will be influenced by this and should become pure as well. This is the PRINCIPLE OF NURTURING THE INTERIOR FROM THE EXTERIOR. For this reason, you wipe the rooms of your house clean of dust and dirt, and order your menservants to sweep the front garden clean every day. You yourself should wipe the dust from your desk from time to time and, going down into the garden, sweep away the dust and dirt.

Keeping the mind clean and the body moving are both aids in nurturing your health.

The principle of Heaven is that first there is yang, and second, yin. Yang objects are few in number, yin are many. There is a paucity of fire but an abundance of water. Fire is easily extinguished, but water is difficult to dry up. Human beings are in the class of yang and are few in number; the birds, beasts, insects, and fish are in the class of yin and are in great abundance. For this reason, it is a natural principle that yang elements are few, while yin elements are many. The few are exalted, while the many are not. True gentlemen[66] are of the yang element and are few, while men of small caliber are of the yin element and are many.

In the Way of Change,[67] the yang is considered good and exalted, while the yin is considered bad and is looked down on. Thus, the gentleman is exalted while the man of small caliber is not.

Water is of the yin element. During the hot months, it should decrease, but instead it increases. During the cold months, it should increase, but instead it dries up and decreases. During the spring and summer, the yang *ch'i* flourishes and so water is produced in abundance. During the fall and winter, the yang *ch'i* changes and so water is scarce.

Should your blood be greatly decreased, you will not die; if your *ch'i* is greatly decreased, however, you will die right away. With sword wounds, vomiting blood, or afterbirth, a person who has lost a great quantity of yin blood will suffer a gradual loss of yang *ch'i* and will die if his blood is given a supplement. If his *ch'i* is given a supplement, his life will be preserved and his blood will increase. The ancients said, "When there is a loss of blood, replenish the *ch'i*. This is the method of the sages of old."

The yang of man's body is always scarce and is exalted, while the yin is always plentiful and is deplored. Thus, we should exalt the yang and attempt to make it flourish. The yin we deplore and try to suppress.

If fundamental *ch'i* is produced, then true yin will also be produced.

If yang flourishes, yin will of itself live long. If you supplement yang *ch'i*, yin blood will be produced of itself. But if you try to supplement an insufficient yin by taking medicines made of *jio*, *chimo*, and *obaku*[68] for a long time and cool and discomfort your body, you will only damage your fundamental yang, weaken the *ch'i* of your stomach, and inhibit the production of blood. In the end, your yin blood will fade away as well.

Now if, in supplementing an insufficient yang, you were to use a toxic medicine like *ubu*,[69] you would encourage a miasmic heat and your yang *ch'i* would be destroyed. So this will *not* supplement yang.

On what classic book is this theory of Superfluous Yang and Insufficient Yin—accorded to Doctor Tan-ch'i[70]—based? I myself have never seen such a book. If these are Tan-ch'i's own words, they are still nonsense and difficult to believe. They go against the principle of the Way of Change, which states that yang is exalted and yin is not. If they are talking about the relative amounts of the distribution of yin and yang, the theory should be called Superfluous Yin and Insufficient Yang. It is simply incorrect to say Superfluous Yang and Insufficient Yin. And what of the people of later generations who will view this offbeat opinion with approval? For the most part, those without proper judgment will be confused by this glib theory and will cling to its one-sided view.

Tan-ch'i was truly a great doctor of the past and made great efforts in medicine. His concentrated efforts in augmenting the yin element were decidedly good for the tendencies of the time. Nevertheless, he was not a medical saint. This is only one of many eccentric theories, and it would be difficult to simply resign yourself and trust in all of them. Between merits and demerits, he sits about halfway. His talent and scholarship should be lauded, but his eccentric theory should not be believed. The kingly and virtuous Way of Medicine does not meander or split into bypaths. It is quite level and ordinary. To go off on the tangent of Tan-ch'i's augmentation of yin is not level and ordinary. You cannot consider it to be the kingly road of medicine.

The fundamental health of men of recent times has gradually waned. If you follow Tan-ch'i's methods and concentrate on augmenting the yin, you will hurt your spleen and stomach and damage your fundamental health. Only Tung-yuan's method of heat augmentation for regulating the stomach and spleen is on the kingly Way of Medicine.

The *Hsien Ch'i Chiu Sheng Lun*, the *Lui Ching*, and other books written by doctors of the Ming dynasty take Tan-ch'i severely to task. And their theories are quite reasonable. But these books are also biased in one sense: they make light of Tan-ch'i's strong points as well. This is called "over-bending the bent parts in order to straighten them." Generally, the sayings of the medical technicians of the past are frequently cranky. In recent times, the doctors at the end of the Ming dynasty were especially given to this weakness. You must pick and choose. Only Li Chung-tzu's theories were extraordinarily correct.

Food, Drink, and Sexual Desire

General Remarks

108

Though your body receives its fundamental health from Heaven and Earth, without the nourishment provided by food and drink your fundamental health would be starved off and it would be difficult to preserve your life.

Our fundamental health is the very foundation of life. Food and drink are the nourishment of life. For this reason, the nourishment received from food and drink should be considered a special daily supplement to man's life and cannot be neglected for even half a day.

However, even though food and drink supply man's essential nourishment, they are also the objects of great desire. They are what the mouth and stomach crave. By giving in completely to these cravings, man can easily go beyond his limits, damage his stomach and spleen, generate a myriad illnesses, and lose his life.

109

When a person is born, the kidneys are considered the most fundamental of the five organs. Shortly afterward, the stomach and spleen become the foundation of the five. When that person eats and drinks, the stomach and spleen first receive these nutrients, digest them, and send the pure liquid[1] to the organs and viscera. The organs and viscera receive this nourishment from the stomach and spleen just as the grasses and trees grow by means of the *ch'i* of the Earth.

For this reason, in the Way of Nurturing Life it is essential to first regulate the stomach and the spleen. Regulating the stomach and the spleen is, indeed, the very first affair in taking care of the body. It is said that the ancients also set limits to their food and drink, and this nourished their health.

110

The ancients said, "Disasters go out through the mouth and disease comes in through it." You must constantly be circumspect about what goes in and out of your mouth.

111

The laws of eating and drinking of the sage Confucius, noted in the tenth chapter of the *Analects*, contain the essentials of nurturing health.[2] This is the way the sages avoided becoming ill. You should consider it to be the proper method.

112

Rice should be well cooked, soft to its very center. You should avoid rice that is hard-boiled or viscous. Rice is good while still warm. Soup is good while hot. Wine should be warmed even in summer. Chilled drink will injure the stomach and spleen. But you should not drink something too hot even in winter. It will inflate your *ch'i* and diminish your blood.

113

For the most part, it is preferable for food to be light and simple.[3] You should not eat a lot of food that is fatty or oily. Raw, cold, and hard or brittle foods should be anathema. Soups are the very best. Meats are also excellent. It is good to stop with only one or two side dishes.

114

The purpose of food and drink is to extinguish hunger and thirst. Once they are extinguished, you should not desire anything more. You should not simply indulge your appetites. The person who indulges his desire for food and drink is forgetting his duty. We call such a person a "mouth-and-stomach man," and he should be regarded with contempt.

If you eat excessively and then help your digestion along with medicine, the *ch'i* of your stomach will be afflicted by the strength of the medicine and the harmony of newly developing *ch'i* will be damaged.

You must understand how important this is. You must consider these things when you eat and drink. You must control yourself and set limits.

When you encounter something pleasing to the mind[4] or agreeable to the mouth, you should first admonish yourself, be mindful of not going beyond limits, and not be willful. If you do not use the power of your mind, it will be difficult to overcome your desires. To overcome your desires, you must use strength.

In showing respect for disease, you must feel some intimidation. You may define intimidation as "cowardice."[5]

115

When it comes to rare or beautifully prepared foods, you should stop eating to a point where you are seventy to eighty percent satisfied. If you give yourself over to complete satiety, disaster will follow. If you can control your desire for a short while, there will be nothing to regret at a later date.

Eating and drinking small amounts and savoring them will give you the same pleasure as eating and drinking to full satisfaction, but without any ill aftereffects.

In all things, if you do them to full satiety, they will surely turn to misfortune. But fully satisfying your appetites for food and drink should be avoided at all costs. Again, if you are circumspect at first, there will be no disasters at a later date.

116

Unbalanced partiality for the FIVE TASTES—spicy, sour, salty, bitter, and sweet—means eating too much of one of them. If you eat a lot of sweet foods, your stomach will swell and be painful. If you are excessive with spicy foods, your *ch'i* will inflate or decrease, you will get boils, and your eyes will become weak. If you have too much salty food, your blood will desiccate, your throat will become parched and, if you drink a lot of water, will become moist and damage your stomach and spleen. If you eat a lot of bitter food, you will harm the vitality of your stomach and spleen. If you take in too many sour foods, your *ch'i* will contract. With the various meats and vegetables, if you continue eating the same thing, they will stagnate inside you and cause harm.

If you provide yourself with the five tastes but partake of them little by little, you will not invite illness.

Food nurtures the body and should not become a means of damaging the body. Thus, you should always choose food that is nourishing and has a beneficial quality. If it has no benefit and is indeed harmful, you should not eat it *even* if it tastes good.

A food that helps to warm the body and does not obstruct *ch'i* is beneficial.

The following foods are harmful:

+ Those that are cold in quality and encourage vomiting
+ Those that block the flow of *ch'i*
+ Those that inflate the stomach
+ Those that are spicy and hot

A person who does nothing but eat and drink is not respected by others. Mencius described this as nurturing the small while forgetting the great.

A person with this tendency is led by the desires of his mouth and stomach, and forgets principle. He fills himself to satiety. His stomach swells and hurts, he becomes ill, and, finally, he grows disheveled in drink. Such a person is to be bluntly despised.

There are FIVE CONSIDERATIONS to bear in mind when eating a meal.

The first calls for you to recognize the source of your food. When you were young, you received your nourishment from your father; when you grew up, you owed this to your lord. You should think this through and never forget it. If not from your lord or father, you received your nurturing from your brothers and sisters, your relatives, or from others. Even now, you should think of where your food comes from and never forget these blessings. The farmers, artisans, and merchants, who eat through their own efforts, should consider the debt they owe to their country.

The second consideration calls for you to acknowledge the sympathy you should have for the hard labor of the farmers and the pains they went through to produce your food. You cannot forget this. You yourself do not till the fields, but live in comfort and ease; yet you receive this nourishment. You should take pleasure in this fact and not just take it for granted.

The third consideration calls for you to recognize the great good fortune you have in receiving this delicious food even though you may have no particular genius, virtues, or righteous behavior, and have made no great efforts to help your lord or to govern the people.

The fourth consideration calls for you to remember that there are many people in the world much poorer than you. They have nothing more with which to be satisfied than a meal of dregs and rice bran. There are also people who die of hunger. You, however, will eat delicious grains to the very end and will never worry about starvation. Is this not a great blessing?

The fifth consideration calls for you to think about ancient times. In great antiquity people did not possess the five grains[6] but staved off hunger by eating the nuts, fruits, leaves, and roots of the grasses and trees. Even after they had the five grains, they did not know how to cook them. Without kettles and pots, they could not boil their food and so chewed the grains raw. Thus, their meal had no taste and damaged their intestines and stomachs.

Today we boil white rice until it is soft and eat it as we please. *And* we have soups and side dishes both morning and night. More than this, we have wine and *amazake*[7] to delight our hearts and aid our blood and vitality.

This being so, at every meal we eat we should repeatedly think over at least the first and second of these five considerations and never forget them. If we do this, those thoughts themselves will give us pleasure day by day.

These are only my own foolish conjectures. I record them here arbitrarily. In Buddhism, there are the Five Views[8] at mealtime, but these are not the same.

119

The evening meal is more easily obstructed and less easily digested than the morning meal. It is better that you eat small quantities for the evening meal. You should eat light, simple, and plain fare. It is not good to have a great number of side dishes with your evening meal. It is not good in general to eat a lot of side dishes. Fish and fowl with a strong taste, or greasy and heavy foods are not good for evening meals. The passage of vegetables such as yams, carrots, turnips, potatoes, and arrowhead bulbs is easily blocked, and they obstruct the flow of *ch'i*. You should not eat a lot of these vegetables for an evening meal. Not eating at all in the evening is your best option.

120

You should avoid all of the following:

+ Rice that has gone bad
+ Rotten fish
+ Macerated meat
+ Foods that have lost their color
+ Foods that smell bad
+ Foods that no longer taste freshly boiled
+ Foods that have not yet ripened
+ Roots that have been dug out before they are fully grown
+ Foods that have passed their prime

The *Analects* of Confucius notes that these foods were not eaten by sages, and such men made a point of taking care of themselves. You should make such guidelines your own rules.

It is also said that even if you have a lot of meat close at hand, you should not eat so much that it overcomes the *ch'i* of rice. You should not eat a lot of meat anyway. A meal has its foundation in rice. Nothing should be more in quantity than rice, regardless of the meal.

121

If you do not have enough rice, you will not satisfy your hunger. Even if you feel that you have not eaten your fill of meat, what you have eaten will be sufficient. If you feel that it was enough, you have over-eaten. You will nurture your *ch'i* by eating your meals in small portions. Vegetables will supplement an insufficiency of grains and meat and are easily digested. Each food has its own reason to be eaten. Nevertheless, you should not eat large amounts.

Your body is the foundation of your fundamental health. If fortified by the nutritious grains, your fundamental health will continue on vigorously. Grains and meat will aid your fundamental health as long as you do not eat them to excess.

If your constitution can digest grains and meat, you will live long. If grains and meat overwhelm your fundamental health, your life will be short. Moreover, the ancients said, "You should eat more grains than meats [thus letting the grains' effect on your digestion overcome the effect of meats], rather than the other way around."

122

You should write down all the things that consistently make you ill, then avoid them. A consistent malady will become a chronic illness. There are foods that will make you ill immediately. Others will do so after some time has passed. You should avoid the latter as much as the former.

123

If you are made ill by some injurious food, you should either stop eating and drinking or decrease your usual portion by half, or perhaps two-thirds. If you are affected by food poisoning, you should quickly get into a comfortably hot bath. You should not eat the salted flesh of either fish or fowl, raw vegetables, oil or fatty foods, sticky foods, brittle foods, rice cakes, or dried or raw sweets.

124

If you have not yet digested your morning meal, you should not eat at noon. Neither should you eat snacks. If you have not yet digested your noon meal, you should not eat an evening meal. If the food you ate the night before has not yet passed through you, do not eat the following morning.

If you cannot bypass mealtime altogether, content yourself with a half portion, and avoid meat and wine.

Generally speaking, there is nothing like fasting to treat a food-related illness or discomfort. If you do *not* fast, a medicine should not be used for light discomfiture.

People who do not understand the Way of Nurturing Life—especially ignorant housewives—will quickly recommend a meal, even for indigestion, and so compound the condition.

Sticky rice gruel is especially injurious. Such cures should not be recommended arbitrarily. Depending on the illness, but especially for food poisoning, not eating for one or two days will cause the patient no harm. This is because the poison will not have passed through; the stomach will still be full.

125

You should not eat either overcooked or undercooked rice. When you boil fish, it is bad not to boil it sufficiently. But when you over-boil food, it loses its flavor and will be easily obstructed inside of you. There is a proper and appropriate way of doing things.

When you steam fish, even if you do so for a long time, it will not lose its flavor. If you boil fish and use a lot of water, it will have no flavor at all.

These things are all mentioned in the *Hsien Ch'ing Yu Chi* by Li Li-weng.[9]

The desire for food and drink arises day and night, and for this reason there are a great number of poor people. Needless to say, wealthy people are easily brought to ruin by extravagant cuisine.

After middle age, our fundamental health wanes, and the sexual desire of both men and women declines. But their desire for food and drink does not. Older people have weak *ch'i* of the spleen, and so are easily damaged by food and drink. An old person will suddenly become ill and die, and many times this is due to injurious food.

You must be circumspect.

Among all the various things to eat, we should consume only those that contain a fresh vitality. We should not eat food that is old or smells bad, or food that has changed in color and taste. All of these easily obstruct the *ch'i* and may stagnate in the body.

Foods that you enjoy are pleasing to your stomach and spleen, and so aid your health. Li Li-weng also said that you should consider food that you love preternaturally as medicine. This is certainly reasonable. Nevertheless, to eat large amounts of a food just because you like it will surely damage your health and is more harmful than eating small portions of food you dislike. It is beneficial to consume small amounts of the food that you like.

129

There are five foods you should enjoy eating:

+ pure foods[10]
+ fragrant foods
+ mild and tender foods
+ foods with a light taste
+ foods of good quality

These are beneficial and cause no harm. Foods in contrast to these should not be eaten.

You can find these facts in books from China.

130

If the sensation aroused by a certain food is not pleasing, it will have no nutrition for you. Rather, it will cause you harm. Even if the meal has been prepared especially for you and required a lot of effort, if it doesn't appeal to you, it will probably cause you harm and should not be eaten. Even if you are at a banquet given by another man, you should not eat food that does not appeal to you.

On the other hand, if a food appeals to you but you have not yet digested your previous meal, you should not eat it.

131

Generally speaking, the amount of time necessary for exercising self-control with food and drink is not long. You must only be patient with your desires for a moment. Moreover, the quantity in question is not great. If you simply avoid eating two or three mouthfuls of rice and one or two bites of side dishes, you can avoid harm.

It is the same with wine. If you are a person who drinks a lot, when you use a little self-control and do not get too drunk, you can avoid harm.

132

Being aware of what is pleasing to your stomach and spleen and what is displeasing, you should eat those foods that are pleasing and avoid those that are not.

What are the FOODS PLEASING TO THE STOMACH AND THE SPLEEN? Warm foods, soft foods, well-cooked foods, foods that are not brittle, foods with a light taste, foods that have not lost the taste of being freshly cooked, clean foods, fresh foods, foods with a pleasant aroma, foods of a mild quality, foods that do not lean too much toward one of the five flavors. These are all foods pleasing and nutritious to the stomach and spleen. These are the foods you should eat.

133

FOODS DISPLEASING TO THE STOMACH AND SPLEEN are raw foods, chilled foods, brittle foods, sticky foods, damaged and unclean foods, rotten foods, boiled but not fully cooked foods, over-boiled foods, foods that have lost the flavor of being fresh boiled, foods boiled and then left for too long, unripe foods, old foods that have lost their true flavor, foods that lean too much toward one of the five tastes, oily foods, and foods with a heavy taste. These foods are displeasing and damaging to the stomach and spleen. These are foods that you should not eat.

134

Being excessive with food and wine, eating and drinking at inappropriate times, eating raw or chilled foods or foods of poor quality that make you ill, and getting diarrhea often—these activities will certainly decrease the stomach's *ch'i*. If you eat such foods time and time again, you will debilitate your fundamental health and shorten your life.

You should be circumspect.

135

Whether you eat one slice of meat or one mouthful of fruit, the taste is the same as if you had eaten ten slices of meat or one hundred mouthfuls of fruit. Rather than eat a lot and ruin your stomach, eat just a bit and appreciate the taste. It is much better not to cause damage to yourself.

136

When a man leaves his hometown, the water and earth of his new residence are different and, unaccustomed to these changed elements, he may fall ill. At such times, if he eats tofu, his stomach and spleen will be easily put in order. This can be found in the notes of Doctor Li Shih-chen's book, *Shih Wu Pen T'sao*.[11]

Good Habits, Bad Habits

137

If you must eat at night, do so early. Avoid eating late at night. Lie down only after the food and drink have been digested and the *ch'i* of this nourishment has circulated well. Lying down too soon will bring on illness.

Generally speaking, we do not move our bodies so much at night, the nutrition of food and drink is not put to use, and so even if we remain somewhat hungry it does no harm. If eating at night is unavoidable, it is better done early and in small amounts.

You should not drink wine at night. If you do so, you should drink early and in small quantities.

138

It is said among the common people that if you are too restrained in your eating, you will receive less nourishment, become emaciated, and finally collapse. These are the words of men who know nothing about nurturing health. We are born with many desires, so when you reach the point where you think you have restrained yourself too much, that should be just about right.

139

If you encounter a favorite food or find some tasty rarity piled up in great quantities before you, then you should be strictly circumspect about exceeding the proper amount. You should not go beyond your limit, particularly when you are hungry.

140

When finding themselves in front of food and drink, men quite often become avaricious and exceed their limit without realizing it. This is a common habit.

Wine, food, tea, or hot water—for any of these you should stop early. Stop when you are not quite full or when you feel you haven't had enough. This is much preferable to stopping after you have eaten your fill.

After eating or drinking, you will surely feel quite full. But if you feel full *while* still filling your mouth, that satisfied feeling will turn to one of excess and you will become ill.

141

People with weak stomachs and spleens, and particularly old folks, can easily be harmed by food and drink. When they find tasty food and drink before them, they should practice forbearance. They should not exceed their limits. If your mind is weak, it will be difficult to overcome your desires. You need a strong mind.

142

When you eat together with friends and acquaintances and find savory-looking dishes in front of you, it is easy to overeat. Being fully satisfied with food and drink is the source of disaster. You should partake of your meals much as you would view flowers in only half-bloom or drink wine to only light intoxication. But you should not get carried away and forget to give yourself warning.

Giving in to your desires will result in disaster. Going to the extreme of pleasure is the foundation of sorrow.

143

You must not do rough or heavy work after a meal. Nor should you walk quickly along the road. Neither should you mount a horse and go to high, elevated places or walk up steep roads.

After eating and drinking wine, if you are drunk and your stomach is full, you should look up and belch out the *ch'i* of the food and alcohol. Massage your face, belly, and thighs with your hands and circulate your meal's *ch'i*.

After eating, young people should train with the bow or spear, practice with the sword, move the body, and walk. But they should not be excessive with hard exercise.

Old people should also move about appropriately to their own level of *ch'i* and physical capacities.

You should not sit comfortably in one place for a long time with an armrest. Your blood and ch'i will stagnate and you will find it difficult to digest your food and drink.

After eating, you should rinse your mouth several times with hot water or tea. This will purify the inside of your mouth and remove things that might be caught between your teeth. It is not necessary to use a toothpick. At night, you should rinse your mouth with a warm salted tea. This will make your teeth strong. In rinsing your mouth, you should use a middle to lower grade tea. This is the theory of Tung-p'o.[12]

If you eat a lot of melons, other fruits, and raw vegetables, often consume cold noodles, or drink a lot of cold water during the summer months, you will surely be afflicted with fevers and diarrhea during the fall.

For the most part, diseases do not occur without a reason. You should be mindful beforehand.

148

Every morning during the cold months, the ancients would drink a little medicinal wine of a mild quality. After the first day of spring,[13] they said it was better to stop for the year.

149

Early in the morning, if you eat a soft, warm rice gruel, you will nurture your stomach and spleen, warm your body, and generate saliva. This is good especially in the cold months. This is one of the theories of Chang-lai.[14]

150

Morning and night, every time you eat your first bowl of rice, if you drink only soup and do not take any side dishes, you will understand the true flavor of rice, and the taste of your rice will be excellent. Later, you can eat side dishes with the five tastes and this will nourish your *ch'i*. But if you eat the side dishes with the rice from the outset, you will lose the true flavor of the rice. If you eat your side dishes later, you will be easily filled though your side dishes be few. This is good for nourishing the body and good for managing poverty.

If you do not eat a lot of side dishes of fish, fowl, and vegetables, you will know the value of the taste of your rice; but if you eat large amounts of vegetables and meat, you will not truly know the good flavor of rice.

Poor people have few side dishes of meat; they only eat soup with their rice. Thus their rice tastes good and their food does not sit heavily in their stomachs.

151

When the days are short, you should not eat snacks during the day. Even when days are long, it is not good to eat a lot during the day.

152

If you eat something thick and fatty for your morning meal, it is imperative that you eat something light and simple for your evening meal. If the evening meal is rich and oily, the meal on the following morning should be light.

153

You should eat all foods when they are fresh and full of the vitality of yang *ch'i*. They will have nothing harmful in them. But foods that have stood for days and are congested with yin *ch'i* should not be eaten. These contain harmful elements. It is the same with foods that have been over-boiled or that have lost their fresh-cooked flavor.

154

Consider these four points regarding eating and emotion:

+ You should not eat soon after becoming angry.
+ You should not get angry after eating.
+ You should not eat while feeling distressed.
+ You should not become distressed after eating.

If you eat something before food in your stomach has digested, the good attributes of that food will become injurious. You should only eat when your stomach is empty.

When nights are long and extremely cold, if you eat and drink thinking to ward off the chill, you should reduce the wine and rice you consume by several mouthfuls.

Similarly, when you are a guest at an evening get-together, you should reduce the amount you eat and drink during meals prior to the party. If you do this, and eat and drink less that night, you will suffer no damage.

You always feel more like eating at night than you do in the morning. You should not give in to this desire and act as you please.

During your morning and evening meals, if you eat your food with just a little salt, your throat will not become parched and you will not feel the desire to drink a lot of hot water and tea. If you avoid drinking too many hot drinks at this time, you will not develop moisture in your spleen and thus will easily generate *ch'i* in your stomach.

159

You should not eat raw fruit on an empty stomach. Nor should you eat a lot of prepared confectioneries. These will damage the yang *ch'i* of your stomach and spleen.

160

You should not eat a lot when you are tired, as you will inevitably want to lie down afterward. If you lie down immediately after eating and then sleep, your respiration will be blocked and unable to circulate well; it will be difficult to digest your food and you will become ill.

Thus, when you are very tired, you should not eat. You should eat a while after finishing your labors, but only if you are not planning to sleep straightaway.

161

In the *Ku Chin I T'ung*[15] it says the following: "Premature death due to the hundred diseases is mostly connected to eating and drinking. The afflictions caused by eating and drinking surpass those caused by sexual desire."

While you can suppress your sexual desire, you cannot abstain from eating and drinking for even half a day. Thus, there are many cases of people being brought to physical ruin by food and drink. If you eat too much, you will have stomach pains. If you drink too much, you are liable to have thickening of the phlegm.

162

Foods that should not be eaten in great amounts include all kinds of rice cakes, dumplings, rice dumplings wrapped in bamboo leaves, dried sweets, cold noodles, different varieties of noodles, buns filled with bean jam, buckwheat noodles, sugar, *amazake*, *shochu*, red beans, vinegar, soy sauce, carp, mudfish, clams, fresh-water eels, shrimp, octopus, squid, Spanish mackerel, yellowtail, salted fish guts, whale meat, raw *daikon* radish, carrots, yams, Chinese rape, turnips, oily foods, and fatty foods.

Drinking Wine

163

Wine[16] is the nectar of Heaven. If you drink just a little, it reinforces your yang *ch'i*, softens youthful vigor, circulates respiration, drives away depression, stimulates interest in the world, and is greatly beneficial to man. But if you drink too much, there is nothing more damaging. Like water and fire, it can be either beneficial or a disaster.

In the poetry of Shao Yao-fu,[17] it says, "Drinking this fine wine / I'm brought to light intoxication . . ." Li Shih-chen says that this shows a real understanding of the subtlety of wine. To drink a little and become slightly intoxicated—with this approach there are none of wine's disasters. And in understanding the true taste of wine, there are many pleasures.

Many of man's illnesses occur because of wine. People who drink much wine but eat only a little live shortened lives. For them, Heaven's nectar becomes the body's destroyer. How terribly sad!

164

In drinking wine, everyone has his own individual limit. If you drink a little, the benefits are many; if you drink a lot, the damage is great. If even a solemn and serious man enjoys drinking great amounts, he will become improperly absorbed in drink, will suffer instability of his character, and will fall into disorder. Both his words and deeds will seem deranged, and he will no longer resemble the person he was. Such people should come to themselves and look inward with mindfulness.

A person should reflect upon this from the time he is young and give himself fair warning. Parents, too, should warn their children about this.

Whatever you practice for a long time will become part of your character. What becomes a habit is difficult to mend, even over an entire lifetime.

Those who tend to drink only a little by nature, can drink one or two cups, become pleasantly drunk, and enjoy themselves. Their pleasure is the same as that of those who drink a lot.

But drinking great amounts will bring great damage. In a poem by Po Chu-i[18] it says:

> The man who drinks gallons at a sitting
> Vainly seeks respect with all that booze,
> But in being drunk, he differs not from me.
> Laugh and take your leave, Mr. Big-Drinker!
> With the bill for the wine, you've paid everything for nothing at all.

How reasonable this is.

165

Generally speaking, wine should be drunk only *after* the morning and evening meals. You should not drink on an empty stomach, either morning or night. To do otherwise will not fail to cause damage. Drinking wine on an empty stomach in the morning will certainly damage your stomach and spleen.

For the most part, it is not a good idea to either chill or heat wine to near boiling, during either the summer or winter. You should drink it warmed. Hot wine will inflate your *ch'i*; cold wine will thicken your phlegm and damage your stomach.

Doctor Tan-ch'i says that it's good to drink wine chilled. Nevertheless, for people who drink a lot, drinking cold wine will damage their stomachs and spleens. But even people who drink just a little will clog their respiration by drinking cold wine.

Warmed wine will aid your yang *ch'i* and circulate food that has been obstructed. Cold wine does not have these two benefits; unlike warmed wine, it will not aid the yang or circulate the *ch'i*.

When you heat wine too much and spoil its qualities, its taste will change. The same will occur if, after heating the wine, it cools too much and you reheat it. In both cases, the wine will damage your stomach and spleen and should not be drunk.

When offering wine to someone—even someone who drinks quite a bit—if you go beyond that person's limit, you will cause him grief. If you do not know how much a person drinks, you should only offer him a little. If he declines, you should not recklessly press him to drink more, but should quickly cease offering. Even if the amount is not enough and there is some displeasure at how small it is, still there is no damage.

Being excessive will always cause harm. It is deplorable to offer a guest a sumptuous dinner and then recklessly press him to drink wine to the point where you cause him discomfort. You should not be the cause of someone becoming horribly drunk. Even though a host does not particularly press wine on him, a guest is liable to drink a lot more than usual and become drunk. But when a host does not recklessly press wine on a guest, and the guest does not decline what is offered, this is the proper limit of drinking and getting drunk.

This is bringing together each person's happiness, so everyone will be pleased. This is the way it should be.

169

The wine bought in the market contains ash and is poisonous. You should not drink things with a sour taste. Wine that has sat for a long time [and is not meant to be aged] and whose taste has changed is poisonous and should not be drunk. A thick, cloudy wine will stagnate in the stomach and spleen and will obstruct *ch'i*. This also should not be drunk.

You can drink a little pure fine wine after your morning and evening meals and become lightly drunk. If *amazake* has been properly made with pure ingredients and then heated a little, it will offer health to your stomach. But *amazake* should not be drunk chilled.

170

In the book *Wu Hu Man Wen*, the names and ages are given of many men who lived long lives,[19] and it is stated that "all these men reached old age without becoming enfeebled. If you would ask, none of them drank wine."

When I look around my own village, I can see that nine out of ten men who have reached a splendid old age do not drink wine. The long-lived man who drinks a lot of wine is rare. Wine can be a medicine for living long if you drink to only light inebriation.

When you drink wine, avoid sweet foods. After drinking, avoid spicy foods. Thus you can avoid weakening the sinews and bones. After drinking wine, you should not drink *shochu*. If drunk at the same time, it will weaken the bones and sinews and cause agonizing pain.

Shochu[20] is a great poison and you should not drink it in great quantities. Seeing that it ignites easily if you apply a flame to it, you should understand that it contains enormous heat. During the summer when yin withdraws inside your body and you wear your clothing open and loose, alcohol poisoning will show on your skin. Thus, to drink just a little will not be injurious. But you should not drink it at all during other months.

You should not drink a lot of medicinal wines made from *shochu*, as they can affect you like poison. Millet or rice brandy from Satsuma and "fire wine" from Hizen[21] are extraordinarily spicy and hot. You should not drink wine imported from other provinces.[22] Because their quality is unknown, they are suspect.

If you drink *shochu*, you should not eat hot foods. Neither should you eat spicy foods or toasted miso. You should not drink hot water. During times of extremely cold weather, you should not drink heated *shochu*. This will cause great harm. Western European–style wines that are made in Kyoto from *shochu* share the same taboos.

If you suffer from *shochu* poisoning, you should drink a concoction of green peas, sugar, arrowroot starch, salt, *shisetsu*,[23] and cold water. You should avoid warm water.

173

You should not drink tea after drinking wine, as it will damage your kidneys. If you eat mustard or spicy foods after drinking wine, it will weaken your bones and sinews.

Drinking Tea, with a Note on Tobacco

174

There was no tea in Japan during ancient times. It was brought to us from China during the middle ages. After that, it was valued as essential for everyday use. It has a cold nature and so lowers *ch'i* and keeps you from becoming sleepy. Doctor Chen Tsang-chi[24] said that if you drink it over a long period of time, you will lose weight, as fat will be leached away. Mu Chiung, Su Tung-p'o, and Li Shih-chen claimed tea has a nonbeneficial nature. Nevertheless, in today's society, there are many people who drink great quantities of tea from morning to night. If something becomes a habit, how is it not going to cause damage?

As tea is something that chills the *ch'i*, you should not drink a lot of it at one time. In the preparation of *matcha*,[25] tea is neither roasted nor brewed and so is quite strong. Because *sencha*[26] is both roasted and brewed, it is mild. Thus, you should normally drink *sencha*.

Drink a little hot tea after a meal and it will help in the digestion of your food and suppress your thirst. You should not add salt to it as this will damage your kidneys. You should not drink tea on an empty stomach, as this will damage the spleen and stomach. You should not drink a lot of thick tea, as it will damage newly generating *ch'i*.

Tea from China has a strong nature. This is because in its initial preparation, it is not boiled. Weak and sick people should not drink the new tea of the year, as this will invite eye disease, blood in the feces, diarrhea, and other complaints. They should drink such tea from the following New Year. According to the individual, it can be drunk without causing harm in the ninth or tenth months[27] of the year it was picked.

If struck by the deleterious elements of new tea, a person can take such medicines as *kososan*[28] and *fukankin shokisan*,[29] according to the conditions of the patient. Or he can have such things as dried plums, sweet grass, sugar, black beans, or ginger.

175

Tea cools the *ch'i*, wine heats it. Wine inflates *ch'i*, tea lowers it. If you get drunk on wine, you become sleepy; if you drink tea, sleep will be chased away. Their characteristics are opposites.

176

You should not drink large quantities of soups, hot water, or tea. If you do, moisture will be produced in your stomach and spleen, both of which are adverse to overly moist conditions.

177

If you drink just a bit of hot water, tea, or soup, a lively energy will be produced in the stomach and spleen and your complexion will become radiant and beautiful.

178

When you brew medicine or tea, you should be selective about the water. Pure and sweet-tasting water is considered to be good. Using rainwater will give your tea a good taste. Put a clean pot out in the garden when it rains. This is better than ground water. Nevertheless, it does not keep well for a long time. Water from snow is considered to be the very best.

179

The method for infusing tea is first to roast it with a weak flame, and then to infuse it over a strong flame. Infuse the tea using a hard, hot-burning charcoal, which should be kept burning vigorously. When the water is bubbling well, add some cold water. If you use this method, the tea will taste good. You should not use a strong flame to roast tea. Nor should you infuse it over a weak or gentle flame.

All of these things appear in the Chinese book on tea.[30]

180

Throughout the province of Yamato, everyone drinks tea from Nara on a daily basis. They also pour green tea over rice. This they cook while adding such things as red beans, green peas, broad beans, mandarin orange peels, chestnuts, and yam buds. This stimulates the appetite and improves passage through the thoracic region.

181

Around the time of the Tensho and Keicho periods,[31] tobacco had been recently imported from foreign countries. The word "tobacco" (淡婆姑) is not Japanese, but a barbarian word.[32] Recently, it has appeared in a number of Chinese books. It is also called "tobako."[33] In Korea, it is called "southern grass." Among common people it is called *roto*,[34] but this is a mistake. *Roto* is something else.

Tobacco has a poisonous nature. Some people who have tried inhaling its smoke have become dizzy and collapsed. It is said that if you become accustomed to it, it will not cause great harm and will even give you some benefit, but it has many disadvantages and causes illness. Again, there is the danger of fire. If you become used to it, it becomes a habit. And once you indulge in it, it is difficult to stop using it. There is a lot involved in this habit and, with all the labor necessary, the servants will be hard-pressed. The best choice is not to smoke tobacco from the very beginning. For poor people, the expenses are considerable.

Discretion with Sexual Desire

182

In *The Yellow Emperor's Classic on Medicine*[35] it says, "The kidneys are the foundation of the five organs." This being so, the Way of Nurturing Life should emphasize taking care of one's kidneys. In doing so, you should not rely on supplementary medicines. You should simply retain and not diminish your pure and essential *ch'i*,[36] at the same time stabilizing the kidneys' *ch'i* and preventing its stimulation.

In the *Analects* it says, "When we are young, we are vigorous and energetic. [In our youth,] we should be extremely cautious about sexual matters."

You should observe the admonition of the sage. If you give in to youthful vigor and energy, you will surely turn your back on proper etiquette, behave excessively, disgrace yourself, and lose face. Though you may have regrets later on, it will be too late. From the very beginning you should think in terms of not causing yourself remorse and of being strictly mindful of proper manners. Needless to say, expending your pure and essential *ch'i* and diminishing your fundamental health is the basis of decreasing the length of your life. You should have great respect for this fact.

People with a deep desire for sexual intercourse who greatly diminish their pure and essential *ch'i* from the time they are young will suffer a loss of fundamental health in the lower half of their bodies, weaken the foundation of the five organs, and surely shorten their lives, regardless of being born with a vigorous constitution. You should be mindful of this.

Food, drink, and sex are the great desires of human beings. Because it is so easy to simply do as you please, you should be absolutely mindful of these things. If you are not, the true *ch'i* of your spleen and kidneys will diminish, and supplemental foods and medicines will have no effect.

Old people in particular should nourish and maintain the true *ch'i* of their stomachs and spleens and should not rely on the support of supplementary medicines.

183

Concerning the periods of sexual intercourse between men and women, Sun Szu-miao says in the *Ch'ien Chin Fang*, "People twenty years of age should ejaculate only once every four days; those thirty years of age, once every eight days; those forty years of age, every sixteen days. People the age of fifty should ejaculate only once every twenty days, while those of sixty should retain their vitality and not ejaculate at all. If people of this age have a vigorous physical strength, they can ejaculate once a month. If a person of extraordinary energy and vitality suppresses his sexual desire and restrains himself by going without ejaculation for a long time, he may suffer boils and tumors. After passing sixty years of age, if his sexual desire does not arise, he should be able to retain [his vitality] and not experience ejaculation. If people who are young and vigorous forbear and ejaculate only twice a month, and if their sexual desire does not arise [frequently], they will be long lived."

Thinking this over now, what is written in the *Ch'ien Chin Fang* offers a broad general principle. But people who are congenitally weak or who eat sparingly and have little strength should value their pure and essential *ch'i*. Such people should have intercourse only rarely, regardless of the above rules. If your mind is permeated with sexual desire, it becomes a bad habit that never ends. You should hesitate before extravagant circumstances, as in the end you may lose your life. Be mindful of this.

There is some meaning in the fact that nothing is said in the *Ch'ien Chin Fang* about sexual relations for people under the age of twenty. Before the age of twenty, blood and *ch'i* have not yet stabilized, and if ejaculation is frequent at this time, it will damage the *ch'i* that *has* been generated, and the very foundation of one's life will be weakened.

184

Young and vigorous people should be strictly circumspect concerning sexual desire between men and women, and make few mistakes in this regard. If sexual desire is not aroused, the kidneys' *ch'i* will not be over-stimulated.

You should not drink sexual stimulants like *uzubushi*[37] in order to be manly in the bedroom.

185

In the *Ta Sheng-lu*[38] it says, "The pure and essential *ch'i* of young men who have not reached the age of twenty is still insufficient, but it is easy for them to excite their sexual desire." They should be absolutely circumspect about sexual intercourse.

186

In the *Ch'ien Chin Fang*, Sun Szu-miao explains how to compensate for insufficiencies in the bedroom. "When a man reaches forty years of age," he says, "he should put these bedroom techniques into practice." His explanations are extremely detailed, but their gist is as follows.

After the age of forty, a man's vigor gradually declines. He should have sexual intercourse fairly often, but simply without ejaculating his pure and essential *ch'i*. If he will do this, his fundamental health will not decrease, his blood's *ch'i* will circulate, and insufficiencies will be compensated.

When I consider the secret meaning of what Sun Szu-miao is saying, it seems to be that beyond the age of forty, the *ch'i* of a man's blood has not yet declined and, as he is not like a withered tree or dead ashes, his sexual desire is difficult to contain. Nevertheless, if he ejaculates his pure and essential *ch'i* often, this will greatly expend his fundamental health, and this is not good for an older man. Thus, a man over forty should have sexual intercourse often, but without ejaculating his pure and essential *ch'i*. The *ch'i* of the kidneys gradually declines after the age of forty. But if he does not ejaculate, his pure and essential *ch'i* will not be perturbed or stagnate as it would for a young man.

If you put this technique into practice, it is easy to fulfill sexual desire without ejaculation. Thus, this is an excellent method for circulating *ch'i* while preserving your pure and essential *ch'i*.

The blood's *ch'i* does not decline radically after the age of forty, so it is difficult to contain the onset of sexual desire. If you *do* contain it, it may in fact cause harm. But if you ejaculate frequently upon getting older, the harm from that could be great as well. The intention here is probably to practice this method according to the situation, thus cooling your sexual desire while reserving your pure and essential *ch'i*.

Accordingly, if you do not expend your pure and essential *ch'i*, you will lose neither your energy nor your *ch'i* though you have intercourse often, and you will not be suppressing your sexual desire of the moment. This teaching of the ancients is an excellent method for not having to suppress a sexual desire that is difficult to put out, and at the same time preserves your pure and essential *ch'i*.

Even though we take the nourishment of the stomach and spleen as the foundation of the human body, if the *ch'i* of the kidneys is stable and vigorous, the fire in the *tanden*[39] will rise and make the *ch'i* of the spleen temperate and plentiful. Thus, the ancients said, "There is nothing like replenishing the kidneys in order to replenish the spleen."

From the time a man is young, he should value his pure and essential *ch'i*, and after the age of forty, he should preserve it more and more, avoiding ejaculation. This is the Way to preserve the very origin of life.

This method is the secret of what Sun Szu-miao taught for future generations. Although it is stated clearly in the *Ch'ien Chin Fang*, people in later times did not know that such techniques cause no harm and in fact are beneficial for preserving one's health.

Even such a great doctor as Chu Tan-ch'i took a narrow view of this technique. He had no faith in it because he did not understand the true meaning of Sun Szu-miao's theory. In his criticism of this excellent theory, Chu Tan-ch'i said, "Without the mind of a sage or the mettle of a Taoist hermit-wizard, it is not easily accomplished. If tried out in the bedroom, it would probably kill a number of people." This, he stated in the *Ko Chih Yu Lun*.

Sages and Taoist hermit-wizards are hard to come by in this world, so if things were, indeed, as Chu Tan-hsi stated, this method would be difficult to practice. But there are a number of things one can doubt about Chu Tan-hsi's theories. He was a great scholar and a learned specialist, but it could be said that his views were somewhat off-kilter.

There is no harm when sexual desire does not arise and the *ch'i* of the kidneys is not disturbed. But if sexual desire *is* aroused, the *ch'i* of the kidneys is disturbed and the pure and essential *ch'i* is held back and not ejaculated. At such times, the *ch'i* will stagnate in the lower half of the body and boils and sores may result. In such instances, if you quickly take a comfortably hot bath and warm the lower part of your body thoroughly, the stagnating *ch'i* will circulate, there will be no blockage at all, and you will not have to worry about boils and the like. This technique is good to know.

There are a great number of taboos for the bedroom. You should be especially respectful of extraordinary phenomena in Heaven and Earth. You should not engage in sexual intercourse during eclipses of the sun and moon, during lightning and thunder, strong winds, heavy rains, intense heat or cold, rainbows, or earthquakes. When the first sounds of thunder ring out during the spring months, sexual relations between husband and wife are taboo. Again, concerning actual location, you should be generally respectful in front of sacred places. You should refrain from sexual relations beneath the sun, moon, or stars, before a Shinto shrine, before the mortuary tablets of your ancestors, or before a statue of the sage.[40]

There are also times of proscription concerning your own physical condition. You should not have sexual intercourse during or immediately after an illness, while you have not yet fully recovered, or particularly after suffering typhoid fever, an epidemic-linked illness, or the ague while the boils and such have not yet healed. You should also refrain from sex when your *ch'i* is depleted, after working to exhaustion, when extremely hungry or thirsty, when very drunk or stuffed with food, after becoming tired from intense labor or a long journey on foot, or while you are angry, sad, anxious, or surprised. During the five days before and the ten days after the winter solstice, you should rest and not allow ejaculation of your pure and essential *ch'i*. Again, sexual intercourse is taboo while a woman's period has not yet finished.

These proscriptions are for the sake of being respectful and circumspect toward the gods of Heaven and the gods of Earth, and for the sake of being mindful of disease in respect to your own body. If you are not mindful of these things, you will invite the punishment of the gods and shorten the term of your own life. Moreover, the children born to you may not be healthy in either body or mind, or may be deformed in some way. There may be disaster but never good fortune.

As to prenatal care, the ancients' rule was to be circumspect about sex from the time a woman becomes pregnant. But the above taboos of the bedroom are antecedent to the problems of prenatal care.

You should be extremely respectful of what the gods of Heaven and Earth observe, and be fearful of the disasters that may be visited upon you and your wife and even your child. Such taboos must be understood before the process of prenatal care.

189

You should not have sexual intercourse while holding back a full bladder. You should not engage in sex after having taken refined Sumatran camphor or musk.[41]

190

In the *I Hsueh Ju Men*[42] it says, "After a wife has become pregnant, you should not have sexual intercourse and fan the flames of desire."

The kidneys are the foundation of the five organs, while the spleen is the fountainhead of nourishment. This being so, the body has its source in the kidneys and spleen. They are like the roots of the grasses and trees. You must maintain and nourish them, and make them stable and strong. If the foundation is solid, the body will be at ease.

Chapter

3

Foodstuffs

Good Food, Bad Food

Once congested with yin *ch'i*, all foods will be harmful and should not be eaten. This is noted in the tenth chapter of the *Analects*.[1] All the foods that the sage Confucius would not eat were those that had lost their yang *ch'i* and become fundamentally yin.

When you put a lid over grains or meat and some time passes, the taste changes because their *ch'i* is congested with yin. With fish or fowl, if a long time passes and it is treated with salt and allowed to stand again for some time, the color, aroma, and taste will change. In both of these cases, the yang *ch'i* is lost.

If vegetables are allowed to stand for a long while, they will lose their vitality and the taste will change. All such foods become yin foods and are injurious to the stomach and intestines. And again, even those that do not cause injury will not be nutritious.

Freshly drawn water and the like are full of yang *ch'i* and have vitality. But if a long time passes, they will become yin and lose their vitality. No food or drink should be consumed if it has lost its vitality and its taste, aroma, and color have changed *even a little*.

If something is dried and has lost its color but is seasoned with salt and is not damaged, it will not have become yin and can be eaten without harm. Nevertheless, when dried foods have had their *ch'i* extracted, even when encased in salt for a long time, they will lose their color, aroma, and taste and become yin. These should not be eaten.

193

During the summer months, foods that have had a lid placed over them while still warm and are allowed to stand for a long time will become steamed and congested in their own heat and will take on a bad taste. Such things should not be eaten.

In the winter months, vegetables that have been struck by frost or that have sprouted beneath the eaves of the house should not be eaten.

All of these are yin foods.

194

There are a great number of foods that are not to be eaten together. I record here the essentials.

When eating pork you should avoid ginger, buckwheat noodles, coriander, dried peas, plums, beef, venison, soft-shelled turtle, crane, and quail.

With beef, you should avoid eating millet, leeks, ginger, and chestnuts.

When eating rabbit, you should avoid ginger, mandarin orange skin, mustard, chicken, venison, and otter.

With venison, you should avoid eating raw vegetables, chicken, pheasant, and shrimp.

With chicken and chicken eggs you should avoid eating mustard, garlic, raw onions, glutinous rice, apricots, fish soup, carp, rabbit, otter, soft-shelled turtle, and pheasant.

When eating pheasant, you should avoid buckwheat noodles, Jew's ear, walnuts, crucian carp, and catfish.

With wild duck, avoid walnuts and Jew's ear.

With domestic duck, avoid apricot and soft-shelled turtle.

With sparrow, avoid apricots and salted meat.

With crucian carp, avoid mustard, leeks, sweets, venison, celery, chicken, and pheasant.

When eating fish sushi, avoid miso, raw barley, garlic, and green peas.

With soft-shelled turtle, avoid amaranthus greens, mustard greens, plums, and domestic duck.

When eating crab, avoid persimmons, mandarin oranges, and Chinese dates.

With apricots, avoid honey.

With bitter oranges and mandarin oranges, avoid otter.

With Chinese dates, avoid leeks.

With loquats, avoid hot noodles.

With arbutus, avoid raw onions.

With all melons, avoid oily dumplings and rice cakes.

With millet and rice, avoid honey.

Cooking green peas with Japanese nutmeg can cause death.

With bracken, avoid amaranthus.

Do not cook dried bamboo shoots with sugar.

Do not cook carp with beefsteak plant, *shiso* stems, or *shiso* leaves.

With catfish, avoid melons and cold water.

With vinegared meat, avoid white muskmelon. Hair on vinegared meat is not healthful.

With miso and raw barley, avoid honey.

You should not eat pepper with plums, apricots, or arbutus.

Finally, it is said that pumpkin should not be eaten together with catfish.

195

Foods that the common people should not eat include raw and cold foods, hard foods, unripe foods, sticky foods, foods that are old and whose taste has changed, foods the preparation of which is not appealing, salty foods, foods with too much vinegar, foods that have lost their fresh-cooked flavor, foods that smell bad, foods with bad color, foods whose taste has changed, old fish, macerated meat, tofu that is several days old, tofu that tastes bad, tofu that has lost its fresh-cooked taste or has been chilled, noodles garnished with oil, anything that has not been fully boiled, wine that contains ashes, foods that have not been cooked long enough, and foods that have already passed their optimum time. You should not eat pheasant during the summer.

The following all contain injurious elements: the hard flesh of fish and fowl, foods with large amounts of oil, foods that taste very fishy, any fish where the condition of one of the eyes is different (implying a disease), the flesh of an animal with red marks on its belly, any bird that did not die naturally and has its feet drawn up, the flesh of any animal that has been shot with a poison arrow, any bird that died from eating poison, desiccated flesh, foods that have become wet from water dripping off a roof, flesh that has been stored inside a rice container, and broth made from meat that has been stored in containers that close in the *ch'i* of that broth. Meats, dried meats, and salted meats that have gone through the summer should not be eaten.

Meat, Fish, and Fowl

196

You should not eat two different kinds of meats at one sitting. And again, you should not eat too much meat. You should not continually eat raw meat, as it tends to stagnate in the body. If you have a soup that contains meat, it is better not to have meat as a side dish.

Meat or dumplings that have been previously broiled can be dipped for a moment in boiling water. Thus, the injurious effects of the flame will be removed, and the food can be eaten. If not prepared in this way, your saliva will desiccate, and this often brings on maladies of the throat.

The hard meat of birds and beasts can be boiled in either soy sauce or miso, and then boiled a second time the next day in the same sauce. If this is done, even thick-cut slices will become soft and taste good. Such meat will not become obstructed in passage. *Daikon* radish may be prepared in the same way.

199

More so than small fish, big fish containing large amounts of oil will easily obstruct the digestive tract. If eaten in thinly cut slices, however, there will be no obstruction. If large carp are cut into thick slices, or if their entire bodies are boiled, they will block *ch'i*. Such fish should be cut into thin slices.

If vegetables such as *daikon* radishes, carrots, pumpkins, turnip,[2] and the like are cut into thick slices and boiled, they too will easily obstruct the digestive tract. They should be thinly cut and boiled.

200

If fresh fish is eaten after being prepared well by enhancing its taste, it will be quickly digested and will not be obstructed in passage. This is due to its vitality. Fish that is over-boiled, oily fish that has been dried, or fish salted for too long will lose its vitality and become a yin food. It will easily stagnate within the body. You should not be ignorant of this principle and think that salted fish is better than fresh fish.

201

You should not eat fish that is oily or that smells "fishy." The guts of a fish contain much oil and should not be eaten. Salted fish guts in particular tend to be obstructive and generate phlegm.

202

Sliced raw fish and *namasu*[3] should be eaten with discretion according to the person. The use of too much vinegar should be avoided. A person who feels cold by nature should eat food that has been warmed up. Sushi should not be eaten by the old or infirm, as it is difficult to digest. Shrimp sushi contains harmful elements. Eel sushi is difficult to digest. Neither should be eaten. The skin of large birds and the thick skin of fish are brittle and oily. They are difficult to digest and should not be eaten.

203

Fresh fish can be eaten if it is prepared nicely with a thin seasoning of salt, dried by the sun, and slightly grilled after one or two days. Or it may be cut into thin slices and seasoned with wine. This will not obstruct the spleen. If a number of days have passed, however, it will block the digestive tract.

Cutting carp into thin slices, sprinkling it with black pepper, and boiling it for a long time in miso is called "unclear soup." It is helpful to the stomach and spleen. It is also good for people with weak spleens or sick people with bloody bowel discharge. Large slices will obstruct *ch'i*, which is not good.

Vegetables, Fruits, and Tofu

205

In books on medicinal herbs it is written that eggplant has some disagreeable qualities. It is poisonous and should not be eaten raw. Even boiled eggplant can cause fever accompanied by diarrhea and general high temperatures, and so should be avoided. To avoid illness, peel off the skin, soak it in the rinse water from rice, leave it to soften overnight or for half a day, and then boil it. It can then be eaten without causing harm.

206

For people with weak stomachs, *daikon* radishes, carrots, potatoes, yams, and burdock should be eaten only after having been cut into thin slices and boiled. If such vegetables are cut into large, thick slices, they will not be thoroughly cooked even when boiled and can damage the stomach and spleen.

But even vegetables cut into large pieces will not cause harm if they are boiled once in thin miso or thin soy sauce, left to soak overnight or for half a day, and then boiled again in the same sauce. And they will taste good. Chicken and wild boar should also be prepared like this.

Of all the vegetables, the *daikon* radish is the best and should be eaten all the time. Remove the tough parts of the leaves, boil the roots and the soft parts of the leaves thoroughly in miso, and eat. This aids the spleen, removes phlegm, and circulates the *ch'i*. But eating *daikon* when raw and bitter will reduce *ch'i*. Nevertheless, when undigested food sits heavy on your stomach, eating a little bit will cause no harm.

Various fruits and dried confectioneries cause no harm if eaten after being toasted, and the taste will be excellent. For *makuwa'uri*,[4] you remove the seeds, steam it, and then eat it. The taste is good and it will not damage the stomach.

Persimmons, both ripe and tree-sweetened, should be heated in boiling water without removing the skin, and then eaten. Dried persimmons should be grilled and then eaten. None of these are injurious to people with weak stomachs and spleens.

The *nashi*[5] pear is a midwinter fruit. If you eat it steamed or boiled, its character softens. But it should not be eaten by a person whose stomach tends to be cold.

When *daikon* radish, Chinese rape, yams, potatoes, arrowhead bulbs, carrots, pumpkins, and sweet vegetables such as leeks are cut into large slices, boiled, and then eaten, their passage will be obstructed, *ch'i* will be blocked, and you will suffer stomach pains. Such vegetables should be cut into thin slices. It s also good to add some spices or, according to the food, a little vinegar. The need for a second boiling is noted above.

Again, with foods such as these, you should not eat two or three different kinds at one time. Almost all sweet vegetables will not pass easily through you, so you should not eat them one after another. Nor should you eat raw fish, fatty meats, or foods with a heavy taste one after another.

209

Of all foods, garden vegetables are the dirtiest. It is not easy to quickly remove the manure and filth that have soaked into the roots and leaves over a long period of time. Such vegetables should be eaten only after having been cleaned by getting a water bucket, filling it with water, rinsing them thoroughly, putting a weight on top of them, and letting them sit overnight or for a day, before taking them out and scrubbing the roots, leaves, and stalks with a brush. I have seen this recently in a book written by Li Li-weng. In China, they do not offer the gods vegetables from the garden, but rather wild vegetables from the mountains and streams.

Nevertheless, melons, eggplants, bottle gourds, and winter melons are not unclean, even though they are grown in gardens.

210

Generally speaking, you should not eat any fruit the seeds of which have not yet fully developed. There is a poisonous double kernel inside the seeds of fruit.

211

Melons should not be eaten on days with a cool breeze or on cool, refreshing days during the autumn months. They should be eaten during extremely hot weather.

You should not eat things such as tofu, *konnyaku*,[6] yams, potatoes, arrowhead bulb, or lotus root if they have been boiled in soy sauce and allowed to cool.

Tofu has injurious elements and will block the circulation of the *ch'i*. Nevertheless, if it is boiled when fresh, retains the just-prepared taste, and is topped with ground raw *daikon*, it can be eaten without causing harm.

Spices, Seasonings, and Sauces

Salt, vinegar, and spicy foods—you should not consume a lot of these three tastes. If you *do* eat large amounts of them and quench a dry throat by drinking a lot of hot water, you will produce moisture and damage your spleen.

You should not drink a lot of hot water, tea, or soup.

Things like ginger, hot pepper, black pepper, knotweed, *shiso*, raw *daikon* radish, and long onions will aid the aroma of food, drive away bad smells, eliminate the noxious elements in fish, and circulate your respiration. Thus, you should add to dishes a little of the appropriate spice to kill off unhealthy elements. But you should not eat them in large amounts. Large quantities of spices will decrease your *ch'i*, cause it to rise, and desiccate your blood.

216

If you eat ginger in the eighth or ninth month, you will have trouble with your eyes the following spring.

217

The sages would not eat food that was not cooked in its proper "sauce." This is the Way of Nurturing Life.

A proper sauce is not just a kind of miso. It is the appropriate seasoning that you should add to a food. To give some examples from the present: salt, wine, soy sauce, vinegar, knotweed,[7] ginger, horseradish, pepper, mustard, and *sansho*.[8] All of these are good when added to the appropriate food.

The addition of these sauces suppresses injurious elements in food. It is not just a matter of producing a pleasant taste.

218

Miso of a mild quality will aid the intestines and stomach. *Tamari*[9] and soy sauce have a sharper quality than miso and are not good for people with diarrhea.

You should not consume a lot of vinegar, as it is not good for the stomach and spleen. However, people with stomach pains should take it in small quantities. Thick vinegar should not be consumed in large amounts.

Rice and Water

There are many methods of cooking rice. *Takiboshi*[10] is fine for healthy people. *Futatabi'ii*[11] is good for people whose *ch'i* is too concentrated in either the five organs or the six viscera, or has stagnated somewhere in the body. *Yudori'ii*[12] is good for people with weak stomachs and spleens.

When rice is cooked until it becomes sticky like glue or paste, it will obstruct your *ch'i*. Hard-cooked rice is difficult to digest. New rice has a strong character and is not good for people in a weak condition. In particular, the variety of rice that ripens early agitates the *ch'i* and is not good for people who are ill. Late-ripening rice has a light character, and is fine.

Rice can both nurture man and be his undoing. Thus, you should not eat rice in large quantities. You should determine the proper amount for every meal. Consuming a large amount of rice will damage the stomach and spleen and will obstruct the flow of your primordial *ch'i*. More than other foods, excessive amounts of rice are difficult to digest and can be greatly damaging.

As a guest in someone's home, you may feel that to eat sparingly of the meal your host has so thoughtfully prepared is not very obliging and puts your host's kind intentions to naught. In this case, take half your usual amount of rice and eat from the side dishes bit by bit. If you follow this course, though the side dishes are numerous, you will escape unharmed. If you consume your usual amount of rice *and* consume a lot of the side dishes of fish and fowl, you will surely cause yourself harm.

After the meal, if you add tea, cakes, rice cakes, and dumplings to your fare, or eat an entirely new meal,[13] you will reach total satiety, block the flow of your *ch'i*, and be broken by the food itself. This is because you have gone beyond your usual amount. Tea, cakes, and a repeat course take a meal beyond the proper limits. For this second round, you should confine yourself to small portions.

If you think you will be eating more after the main meal, be sure to cut down on your rice beforehand.

222

You should enjoy water that is pure and sweet. You should not use water that is not pure and has a bad taste. It is an established principle that a man's innate character is different according to the taste of the water in his hometown. Thus, your choice of water is extraordinarily important.

Moreover, you should not drink water that has been polluted, and you must not fail to select good water for boiling medicine or tea.

223

Rainwater that has just fallen from the sky is of good quality. It is good to collect this in jars and boil it for medicine or tea. Water that drips off the roof is extremely poisonous.

You should not drink stagnant water. Neither should you drink water that leaked onto land from stagnant water. You should not allow dirty standing water to remain in the vicinity of a well. You should take steps to prevent water from leaking into a well from the ground.

It is good to let boiled water cool and then drink it after an appropriate amount of time. If you drink water that is not properly boiled, your stomach will swell.

Cooking and Taste

225

Things like *matsutake* mushrooms, bamboo shoots, tofu, and vegetables that have an excellent taste should be cooked alone. To boil them mixed with other foods will spoil their flavor.

In the *Hsien Ch'ing Yu Chi*, Li Li-weng says the following: "If the taste is poor, the food will not suit the stomach or spleen. And it will not be nutritious."

226

When you freshen up rice cakes or dumplings and do not re-boil or grill them for a second time, the meal will be difficult to digest. Rather than steaming them, you should boil them. This will make them soft and easy to digest. After rice cakes have sat for a few days, it is better to eat them only after broiling or boiling.

Thoughts on Overeating and Treatment for Various Illnesses

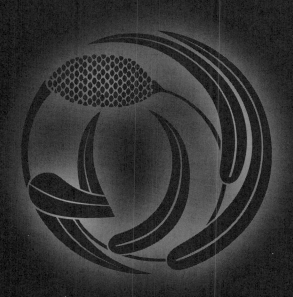

For the Weak, Young, and Elderly

227

People who are weak or who have debilitating diseases should always eat—a little at a time—the flesh of fish or fowl made savory. This is better than supplementing food with *jingi*.[1] Fresh fish of good quality should be well cooked. To salt fish for more than one or two days is excellent, but if prepared in this way for too long, the taste will be ruined. Furthermore, it will not pass through the digestive tract easily. It is also good to eat the flesh of fresh fish that has been cooked after being prepared in miso. But it will not keep long during the summer months.

228

It is good for a person with a weak spleen to eat grilled fresh fish. It will not be any more obstructive than boiled fish. It is good to eat small fish that have been boiled. Eating large fish that have been grilled, cooked after being soaked in wine, prepared with ginger or horseradish, or seasoned in a proper sauce will do no harm.

229

Generally speaking, the stomachs and intestines of the Japanese are weak, so the meat of various animals is not good for them and should not be eaten in large amounts. Squid and octopus should also not be eaten in large amounts as they are difficult to digest. The eggs of chickens and ducks, if hard-boiled, will obstruct *ch'i*, but are fine if they are "fluffy-cooked,"[2] as the common folk say. Both meat and vegetables will obstruct *ch'i* and block the digestive tract if they are cut into thick slices or boiled whole.

230

A person with a weak stomach and spleen who is avoiding raw vegetables should eat dried vegetables that have been boiled. During the winter months, a *daikon* radish may be cut into thin slices and dried for a day just as it is. Lotus root, burdock, and *udo*[3] root may all be cut into thin slices, boiled, and then dried. It is good to dry *shiitake* mushrooms, *shoro* mushrooms,[4] and *iwatake*.[5] *Matsutake*[6] mushrooms should be pickled with salt. It is also good to slice up a *yugao*,[7] pickle it in salt for one night, put it under a press, and then dry it. For sweet potatoes, you pour hot water over the stems and then dry them in the sun. All of these are appropriate foods for weak people.

Foods with a cold quality are not good for the elderly or weak people.

231

Elderly people and people with weak stomachs and spleens should not eat such things as rice cakes, dumplings, meat, or jam buns; nor should they eat brittle or chilled foods. These foods are difficult to digest. Eating things such as dried or unbaked confectioneries should be done with care. According to the occasion and the person, such foods can cause harm. They should be especially avoided after the evening meal.

232

Throughout the four seasons, both the very young and the elderly should eat food that has been heated. Particularly in the summer months, the *yin* lies dormant and within. Even young and vigorous people should eat food that has been heated. You should not eat raw or cold things. Such foods are quick to stagnate inside and readily bring on diarrhea. You should not drink a lot of cold water.

233

Foods that old or weak people should not eat include raw and cold foods, hard foods, unripe foods, oily foods, cold noodles, cold or hard rice cakes, dumplings, rice dumplings wrapped in bamboo leaves, cold buns filled with bean jam and their wrapping, hard cooked rice, raw miso, as well as poorly produced and chilled *amazake*. Whale meat, sardines, tuna, barracuda, and all raw fruits will damage the *ch'i* developing in the stomach and spleen.

234

The people of China and Korea have strong stomachs and spleens. They eat a lot of rice, and even if they eat the flesh of the six beasts[8] this causes no harm. The Japanese are different. If they eat large quantities of grains or meat, they easily suffer collapse. This is because the *ch'i* of the Japanese body is different from that of people from other countries.

On Volume of Consumption

235

If you consume but a little food and drink, there will be an empty space between your stomach and spleen, your fundamental *ch'i* will circulate easily, your food will be digested easily, and everything that you have eaten and drunk will be nutritious. As a result, your illnesses will be few and you will become strong.

If you eat large amounts of food, your stomach will be filled and the path along which your *ch'i* should circulate will be blocked. Without an empty space between your stomach and spleen, your food will not be digested and what you eat and drink will not be nutritious. Instead, your food will stagnate, the path of your fundamental *ch'i* will be blocked, your circulation will be improper, and you will become ill. If this situation becomes pronounced, you will die in great discomfort.

All of this is only because you eat excessively, fill your stomach, block your *ch'i*, and cut off your circulation. Becoming ill or dying suddenly after a meal is a result of this.

Generally speaking, people who eat a lot or drink large amounts of wine live short lives. You should stop such habits right away. And to repeat myself yet again, elderly people have weak stomachs and spleens that are easily damaged by food and drink.

You should not eat and drink excessively. Show some temerity regarding this.

236

Your evening meal should be less in quantity than your morning meal. It is fine if the side dishes of meat are also small.

237

Tung-p'o said, "For meals both morning and night, I do not go beyond one cup of wine and one slice of meat. If I have an honored guest, I add one dish. But though I reduce my own portions, I do not increase those of the guest. If someone invites me out, I let him know about this beforehand. The first reason for this is that if you are contented with your portion, you nurture your happiness. The second reason is if you're easy on your stomach, you nurture your *ch'i*. The third reason is that if you cut down on your expenses, you nurture your assets."

We should follow Tung-p'o's method for the sake of both economy and health.

238

Both morning and night it is better to have just one kind of side dish. Beyond that, you could eat either salted meat, salted chopped meat, or some sort of pickle. As for soups, even the wealthy should have only one kind. You prepare two kinds of soup when you entertain guests, but the second is served only if the guest doesn't take any interest in the first.

A Chinese man by the name of Kao Shih-lang[9] did not serve his brothers two courses of soup or meat, but prepared only one course. Morning and night he himself ate only *fu-p'ao*, which consists of *daikon* radish and bottle gourd. The wealthy and respected Fan Chung-hsuan[10] customarily did not eat a succession of side dishes of meat.

We should make such economy and nurturing our own rule.

Treatments and Illness, with Comments on Overeating

239

When you consume excessive quantities of food and drink and incur the inevitable consequences, you then turn to strong medicine to help sooth your stomach and ease digestion.

149

Suppose that an enemy invaded your domain and, wreaking havoc, attacked your castle in an attempt to destroy it. You would send out strong troops to fight in your defense, and if your soldiers did not kill great numbers of the enemy, a victory would be difficult.

Now, when you enlist medicine to help digestion, your stomach becomes the very battlefield upon which your enemies and allies fight. The wine and food become the enemies attacking your stomach, while the strong medicine, with which you attack the ailment, becomes your ally. In the meantime, your fundamental health decreases.

Enemy and ally battle it out in your stomach, and the harm this does to your fundamental health is more than considerable. Rather than drawing the enemy into battle on your own territory, it would be far better to block its advance and prevent it from entering. If you do not consume excess food or drink, neither can become your enemy and a battle cannot ensue. To start such a battle damages your stomach's *ch'i*. This is quite regrettable.

240

Many people who suffer terribly and die soon after a meal have been excessive in their eating and drinking, have filled themselves completely, and have blocked their flow of *ch'i*.

The first thing to do in such a case is to boil ginger with a little salt, have the patient drink a good amount of this decoction, and have him vomit copiously. After this, it would be good to give him a medicine that will help the obstructed food be digested and circulate the *ch'i*. If apoplexy has been diagnosed, he should not be given *sogoen* or *enreitan*.[11] The result of doing this would be poor. Furthermore, he should not be given the least bit of food right away. In particular, he should not be given something such as a sticky rice gruel, as this would cause his *ch'i* to become increasingly weaker until he dies. It would be fine not to give food for one or two days, since this is a matter of food poisoning. Many people in our country consider it to be apoplexy, and treat it as such.

241

Eating whenever you are hungry or drinking whenever you are dry—that is, giving in to your hunger and thirst and consuming large amounts of food and drink at one time—will fill you completely, damage your stomach and spleen, and ruin your fundamental health.

You should be mindful at moments of hunger and thirst. And again, to quickly eat and drink even more—and more again—before your previously consumed meal has been digested, will block you up inside and cause damage. You should take your meals only when you can enjoy food and drink, having digested what you have previously consumed. In this way, all your food and drink will be nutritious.

242

When you lie down, if the food you have eaten is blocked and you are choked with phlegm, you should take a little medicine to induce the phlegm's elimination. It is a frightful thing to lie down at night and have phlegm obstructing your throat.

243

Depending on the illness, there are certain foods that a person should or shouldn't eat. You need to consider the characteristics of a food and then determine in detail whether it is good or bad according to the particular disease. Again, there are a number of foods that are forbidden a woman during her pregnancy. Such things should be strictly observed.

244

When you are taking medicine for the stomach, you should avoid the following:

+ sweet things
+ fatty foods
+ animal flesh
+ fruit
+ rice cakes
+ dumplings
+ raw or cold foods
+ any foods that will block the circulation of *ch'i*

In addition, if you eat a lot of any one food while you are taking stomach medicine, the medicine will not circulate and it will have no effect. With wine, you should stop at just one cup.

On the day that you take the supplementary medicine, you should especially avoid these things.

Generally speaking, on the day that you are taking medicine, eating light foods will boost the efficacy of the medicine, while eating strong-tasting foods will weaken it.

245

If your stomach is rumbling, or your food is obstructed and you have an unpleasant sensation in your belly early in the morning, you should eat less for breakfast. You should not eat meat, fruit, or foods that will obstruct your *ch'i*. You should not drink wine.

If you still suffer from the effects of alcohol after a heavy session of drinking, you should not consume rice cakes, dumplings, grains of any type, dried candies, fruit of any kind, *amazake*,[12] unrefined wine, fatty foods, sweet foods, or anything that will block the circulation of *ch'i*. You should eat and drink only after the effects of the alcohol have gone.

There are some things that sick people are keen to eat. When they ask for food that could harm them, or for things like cold water, you cannot just give in to their requests. Nevertheless, when a patient is adamant, you can fulfill his request by letting him taste the item but not allowing him to swallow it. This is one of the techniques of nurturing health that actually provides for the patient's wishes.

For the most part, wanting an item of food or drink is a desire of the tongue, not the throat. You chew it, then hold it in your mouth for a moment to savor the taste. Afterward, the taste is the same whether you swallow it or spit it out.

Grains, meats, soups, and wine enter the stomach and nourish the viscera. Foods other than these are not nourishing. It makes no difference if they are not swallowed. We speak of foods that, once eaten, damage the body. But if you spit them out without swallowing them, there is no harm. It is the same with cold water. If you keep it in your mouth for a while, enjoy the taste, and then spit it out, there will be no harm. Water held in the mouth removes heat from inside your mouth and strengthens your teeth.

Nevertheless, people with many desires but no mindfulness are unable to use this method.

When you suffer from diarrhea, from food that has not yet passed through your system, or from stomach aches, bathe in warm water to warm up your body. If you do this, your *ch'i* will circulate and you will recover. This is very efficacious and is much better at the beginning of an illness than taking medicine.

In the past, in China there was an official in charge of dietary medicine. He is said to have treated the One Hundred Diseases by employing the nutrition in foods. Even today, it is necessary to practice treatments that employ dietary nutrition. Old people in particular have weak stomachs and spleens and should eat with nutrition in mind. Taking medicine is only for times when there is no other option.

Acupuncture and Moxa Treatment

What about acupuncture? Acupuncture treatment circulates retarded blood and *ch'i*, disperses food accumulated in the stomach, and eliminates stubborn numbness in the hands and feet. Acupuncture removes excessive *ch'i*, circulates internal *ch'i*, and leads *ch'i* in all directions.

When used for conditions that come on quickly, like obstruction[13] and stomach aches, a treatment that eliminates poison and leads away *ch'i* works faster than medicine or moxa treatment.

If you do use acupuncture in a situation in which there is no obstruction, however, it may decrease the fundamental *ch'i*. Thus, in the *Cheng Ch'uan Tsai Wen*[14] it says that "Nothing is gained from acupuncture if there is a leakage [of *ch'i*]. Nevertheless, if acupuncture treatment can eliminate blockage and circulate *ch'i*, and the patient's system is then not obstructed, food and medicinal supplements can be easily applied."

The Yellow Emperor's Classic on Medicine states, "Do not administer acupuncture for an intense fever. Do not administer acupuncture when the symptoms are not stable, or if the patient is sweating copiously. Do not administer acupuncture to a person who is exhausted or is suffering from intense hunger. Do not administer acupuncture to a person who is suffering from intense thirst, has just eaten to surfeit, or is very excited." It also warns of the following: "Do not administer acupuncture to a person whose character is lacking or whose disease is not grave enough for the treatment." These are the warnings from *The Yellow Emperor's Classic on Medicine*, but all of this is summed up in a statement from the *Cheng Ch'uan Tsai Wen*: "Nothing is gained if there is a leakage [of *ch'i*]."

Over and above these restrictions, you should not receive acupuncture right after a bath or while drunk.

Both the doctor of acupuncture and the patient should understand these admonitions from *The Yellow Emperor's Classic on Medicine* and abide by them.

251

Both benefits and injuries may result from using acupuncture and come more swiftly than from using medicine and moxa treatment. You should be able to weigh these benefits and injuries well.

When acupuncture needles are inserted, they should not induce intense pain, which indicates incorrect application and can be harmful.

Again, if you violate the admonitions mentioned in the books above, *ch'i* may decrease, rise, or move incorrectly. The result will be a worsening of your condition rather than a curing of the disease. You should be careful about this.

252

For the old and infirm, when administering medicine, acupuncture, moxa, *doin*, or massage, you should not apply it roughly in hopes of a quick cure. A rough application is done in hopes of an immediate effect, but taking this approach with the elderly will result in a quick disaster. Even if it feels good at the time, harm will follow.

253

Why is moxa applied to the body? The life of a human being is based on the fundamental *ch'i* received from Heaven and Earth. The fundamental *ch'i* is yang *ch'i*. The yang *ch'i* is warm and belongs to the element of fire. The yang *ch'i* gives life to all the Ten Thousand Things in Heaven and Earth.

The blood, which is yin, is also born from the fundamental *ch'i*. When the fundamental *ch'i* becomes congested and does not circulate, however, *ch'i* decreases and you become ill. The blood also decreases. Therefore, if you borrow the *ch'i* of fire, aid the yang, and supplement the fundamental *ch'i*, the yang *ch'i* is developed and strengthened, the spleen and stomach are regulated, food moves through the system, *ch'i* and blood circulate, and neither food nor drink are blocked. In this way, negative yin *ch'i* is dispersed. Thus, yang is promoted, *ch'i* and blood are invigorated, and disease is eliminated through the power of moxa.

254

When you receive moxa, you should not be exposed to the cold *ch'i* of the wind. If there are strong winds or rain, heavy snow, thick mist, or rainbows, you should postpone your treatment until the weather has cleared up. Emergencies, however, are exempt from these restrictions. You should also avoid sexual intercourse for three days before moxa treatment and for seven days after. Likewise, you should not have moxa treatment for five days before the winter solstice or for ten days after.

255

After moxa treatment, you should eat only light meals and allow your blood and *ch'i* to flow easily and harmoniously. You should not eat large amounts of anything with a strong taste. You should eat no large meals and should not get too drunk on alcoholic beverages. You should not consume hot noodles, chilled food, cold wine, food that causes you to pass gas, or meat that is difficult to digest.

256

You should choose exactly the right spot for moxa treatment. If you apply it many times in a random fashion, your *ch'i* and blood may decrease.

257

There is less *ch'i* in the lower body of old and worn out people. They are constitutionally weak and their *ch'i* can rise quickly. If the moxa treatments they receive are too long or too many, their *ch'i* will rise, the lower parts of their bodies will become increasingly weaker, and their waists and legs will lose their strength. One should be mindful of this.

Chapter

5

The Five Officials

General Remarks

258

The ear, eye, mouth, nose, and body are in charge of their respective duties of hearing, seeing, speaking, smelling, and moving, and so are called the FIVE OFFICIALS.

The mind is the master of the Five Officials. It is in charge of thought and is called the Heavenly Lord. From within, the mind manages the Five Officials. It should think deeply and correct their good and evil. Because of the Heavenly Lord, the use of the Five Officials is enlightened, and it would be unnatural for the Five Officials to use the Heavenly Lord.

If the mind is the master of the body, you will be at ease and without trouble. Then, the Five Officials will receive their orders from the Heavenly Lord, take care of their respective duties, and not simply act as they please.

Living and Working Quarters

259

The place where you usually reside or work should face south, be close to a door, and be nice and bright. You should not constantly be in a dark and gloomy place, as this will block your *ch'i*. However, constantly residing in a place that is too bright will rob you of your spirit. You should find a place halfway between yin and yang, with a balance of light and dark. If it is too bright, you should pull down a bamboo curtain. If too dark, you should roll up the blind.

260

When you lie down, it is better to have your head to the east and thus take in living *ch'i*. You should not lie with your head to the north and inhale dead *ch'i*. If your lord or your father is nearby, you should not lie with your feet in their direction.

When sitting, you should do so with correct posture and not lean to one side or another. When taking a break, you may sit at ease but should not squat. Occasionally sitting on a stool or chair is good for the circulation of *ch'i*. The Chinese do this.

261

Both the rooms in which you reside and the utensils that you use should be simple, clean, and without pretension. The sitting room should keep out cold winds and be a comfortable place to spend time. Your implements should be in accord with their intended use. If you find nothing lacking, then what you have at present should be sufficient. Enjoying luxuries can become a habit. Once greed and extravagance arise, your mind will find itself ill at ease and you will have many distractions. This can only damage the Way of Nurturing Life.

262

If there is the least crevice in the room where you sit or lie down, you should plug it up. A breeze seeping through a crevice or blowing in through some other entry point can easily come into contact with a person's skin and bring on some illness. This is something to which you must pay attention. When you lie down at night, if there is a hole through which the wind passes close to your ear, the hole should be filled.

On Sleeping Well

263

When you lie down to sleep at night, you simply must lie on your side. You should not lie on your back. Doing so will block your *ch'i* and bring on nightmares. You should not place your hands over your chest after you go to sleep. This will block your *ch'i* and will easily bring on troubled dreams. You should be cautious about these two things.

264

When you lie down at night, you should stretch out your legs before falling asleep. But just before going to sleep, you should draw up your legs and lie on your side. This is called the SLEEP OF THE LION. During the night, you should turn over at least five times.

If your thoracic region is filled with *ch'i*, extend your legs and rub your chest and abdomen vigorously with your hands in a downward motion. The person whose *ch'i* is rising should vigorously wiggle his big toes. According to the person's nature, if he does this and yawns repeatedly, he will expel the bad *ch'i* that remains inside of him. However, it is better not to yawn too much or with too great a force.

When you go to sleep, it is better not to lie with your mouth facing down. It is not good to drool while you sleep.

It is not advisable to lie on your back, as this is apt to bring on nightmares. When you lie down, bend your thumbs and grasp them with your other fingers. Thus, you will not unconsciously place your hands over your chest, thereby restricting it, and you will not have troubled dreams. After a while, this will become a habit, and you will not open your hands even while you sleep. You can read about this method in a book called the *Ping Yuan Hou Lun*.[1]

265

If there is phlegm in your throat when you go to sleep, you should expectorate it at all costs. If you go to sleep with phlegm in your throat, you will later have nightmares and troubled sleep. Medical books advise the elderly to take some medicine to clear away the phlegm before they lie down at night. This is for the above-mentioned reason.

For evening and late-night meals, you should not eat things that will produce phlegm and block your *ch'i*. You should respect this in connection with having nightmares.

266

When you lie down at night, your clothing should not cover your face. This will block your *ch'i* and cause it to rise. You should not light lamps when you go to sleep, as neither your yang nor yin *ch'i* will settle. If you must do so, you should set the lamps at a distance and out of sight.

You should close your mouth when you sleep. If you sleep with your mouth open, you will lose your true *ch'i*, and your teeth may fall out prematurely.

267

It is better to get up late in the cold months and early during the hot months. It is not good to sleep in a draft even during the hot months.

It is not advisable to be exposed to the wind as you sleep. Neither is it good to be fanned as you sleep.

Massage, Rubbing, and Other Therapeutic Practices

268

By and large, once a day you should have someone massage your entire body, from your head to your toes, and especially your joints. Each part of your body should be massaged ten times.

First, the top of your head should be massaged; next, around the four sides of your head; third, just behind the eyebrows, and after that at the very edge of your eyebrows.

Pressure should be applied along both edges of the nose, inside the ears and behind the ears. Next, rub from behind the ears down the nape of the neck on both the right and left, applying the right hand to the left and the left hand to the right.

Next, the shoulders, the elbow joints, the lower arms and wrists, and all ten fingers should be manipulated. After that, the back should be pressed down and pounded. Then, you should be massaged from the sides to the back of your hips.

Finally, the chest, breasts, and stomach should be massaged sufficiently, followed by the thighs, knees, shins, calves, ankles, tops of the feet, toes, and soles of the feet. All of these should be rubbed and manipulated with two hands. This is explained in a collection of printed works called the *Shou Yang Ts'ung Shu*.[2]

You can also do this massage yourself.

269

In the *Ju Men* it says that *doin*[3] is one of the methods of preserving your health. Man's mind should always be at peace, but his body should always be moving. If you sit at rest the entire day, you will encourage disease. Sleeping for a long time or sitting at length is far worse than standing or walking for long periods.

270

If you practice the METHOD OF *DOIN* every day, you will circulate your *ch'i*, digest your meals well, and avoid aches in the stomach or chest.

Before you get up in the morning, extend both legs, exhale any impure *ch'i* that remains from the night before, and sit up. Then look upward, join the fingers of your hands, and extend your arms forward and upward. Clatter your teeth for a while as though shivering, and then press the nape of your neck several times—first with your right hand, then with your left. Following this, raise both shoulders, pull in your neck, shut both eyes, and quickly let both shoulders drop. Do this three times.

Next, rub your face with both hands in a downward direction several times. Rub your eyes for a while from the points closest to your nose outward, then rub your nose six or seven times with the middle fingers of each hand. Next, take your earlobes between two fingers of each hand, then rub them and pull them down six or seven times. After this, place the middle finger of each hand into your ears, probing and stopping up the canal. Then remove your fingers.

Now intertwine the fingers of both hands and, as you pull to the left, turn your head to look to the right. Then pull to the right and turn your head to the left. Do this three times.

With the back of your hands, rub both left and right upper sides of your hips diagonally down from the waist ten or so times. Then press down on your hips with both hands. Now rub both the upper and lower parts of your hips with the palms of your hands several times. This will regulate your circulation and lower your *ch'i*.

Next, lightly strike the upper parts of your buttocks ten times or so. Following this, rub your thighs and knees with a downward motion. After that, intertwine the fingers of both hands and grasp one knee. Make as though you are about to extend your foot outward, then pull it in toward you with both hands. Do this a number of times with both feet.

Following this, rub both inner and outer parts of your calves with both hands a number of times. Now, grasping the five toes of the right foot with your right hand, rub the inner sole of your foot with your left hand and then the inner sole of your left foot with your right hand. Do this twenty or thirty times. Pull the big toes of both feet with some strength and lightly twist the other toes as well.

This is the technique of *doin*. A person who has some leisure can do these exercises every day. Of course, you can have your servants or children rub your legs and the soles of your feet, stopping when these places become hot. You can also have them pull your toes.

If you do this morning and night, it will lower and circulate your *ch'i* and keep your feet from becoming painful, and you will become extremely healthy.

You should rub the soles of your feet like this whenever you are going out to walk a great distance, and also upon your return.

271

You should frequently have someone use two hands to rub both the inside and outside of your legs from the knees down. Have him rub the soles and then the upper part of your feet vigorously a number of times, and then pull your toes. If you do this, your *ch'i* will both lessen and circulate well. Doing it yourself is far better. This is an excellent method.

272

When your *ch'i* is circulating properly and you are feeling well, you should not practice *doin* or receive a massage. Moreover, you should avoid massages during the winter months. You can read about this in *The Yellow Emperor's Classic on Medicine*.

When your body is overworked and you are ill with rising *ch'i*, *doin* and massage should be avoided. Certainly, it is good to move your body peacefully at any time throughout the year. This practice is excellent after meals. Rubbing the inner soles of your feet is good at any time.

273

It is advisable to comb your hair often. This is good for the circulation of *ch'i* and will lower a rising *ch'i*. However, the teeth of the comb should not be too fine, as this causes the hair to fall out.

You should frequently clack your teeth together in a light manner. This will make them hard and will prevent cavities.

From time to time, you should warm your hands by rubbing them together and place them over your eyes to warm them as well. This will brighten your vision and prevent eye disease.

You should also rub your face two to seven times from your hairline down to your forehead and face. The ancients said, "Your hands should always be on your face," meaning you should rub your face from time to time. If you do this, your *ch'i* will circulate, a rising *ch'i* will be lowered, and you will develop a beautifully balanced complexion.

You should often rub both sides of your nose and the base of your ears with the middle fingers of both hands.

You should rise at four in the morning, sit down and grasp the toes of one foot with one hand, and rub the sole of that foot with the other hand. You should do this for some time and repeat with the other foot. When the soles of your feet have been warmed by this activity, you should manipulate the toes of both feet with your hands. You can have servants do this for you as well.

Another theory has it that, regardless of the hour, if you do this for some time every time you rise, you will have no problems with your feet. It will lower a rising *ch'i* and ameliorate weak feet, aiding you in the difficulties of standing up. The ancients said that this is extremely efficacious. You can read this in the *Yang Lao Shou Ch'in Shu* as well as in the theories of Su Tung-p'o.

When you lie down at night, you should have a child warm up his hands by rubbing them together and then rub them over the area of your kidneys for some time. Likewise for the soles of your feet. It is also fine to do this by yourself. You should also have a child lightly pat down the area below your kidneys and around your buttocks.

In the *Ju Men* it says, "After the age of forty, when you have no urgent affairs, it is good to press down on your eyes." When you have nothing essential to do, you should keep them closed.

Care of the Body

277

Every night when you are about to go to bed, you should comb your hair vigorously and wash your feet with hot water. This will circulate your *ch'i* well. Also at this time, you should gargle with hot tea to which salt has been added. This will cleanse the interior of your mouth and will make for strong teeth. It is acceptable to use a low-grade tea for this.

278

Generally speaking, wearing clothes that are too warm, sitting by a hot fire, soaking in a hot bath for a long time, eating hot foods, and warming the body too much are deleterious to your health. Your *ch'i* will escape from your body, decrease, and start to rise. This can be of great harm to anyone, and you should take this as a warning.

279

You should not put your feet close to the hearth; it will cause your *ch'i* to rise.

280

When you wait upon a noble or sit in your lord's mansion for a long time, your feet may fall asleep, you may suddenly have difficulty standing, and you may even fall down.[4]

Before you stand, you should wiggle the toes of both feet repeatedly, bending and extending them. If you do this, your feet will not fall asleep and you will not have to worry about not being able to stand.

If on normal days you get into the strict habit of bending and extending the big toes of both feet, you will not have to worry about cramps in your calves. If you do suffer such cramps, wiggle the big toe of your foot and the pain should go away. This is a method of treatment for an emergency, and you should be aware of it.

If a person has rising *ch'i*, he should extend both legs and wiggle his big toes for a while. This method will lower his *ch'i* and is quite beneficial.

281

Tung-yuan said that if you suddenly encounter a cold wind and happen to be dressed in light clothing, you should tense up the *ch'i* of your entire body in order to block off the cold wind and prevent it from penetrating your skin.

282

It is written in the *Liu Ch'ing Jih Cha*[5] that glasses are called *aitai*.[6] They are also called spectacles. You should start wearing glasses soon after the age of forty in order to preserve your eyesight. Glasses made of Japanese crystal are excellent. You should wipe them with silk or a woolen cloth held between two fingers.

Glass is easily broken and inferior to crystal. You should wipe glasses made of glass with a lamp wick.

283

The following is the method for brushing your teeth and washing your eyes.

Every morning, first wash and warm your eyes with warm water, and cleanse the inside of your nose. You should then rinse out your mouth with warm water and expectorate whatever might have remained in your mouth from the day before. Following this, you should rub and brush your upper and lower teeth with dried salt, and then swish warm water around in your mouth twenty or thirty times. While doing this, you should be soaking a rough cloth like a fine sieve in warm water placed in a separate bowl. Then wash your hands and face. Once that is done, spit out the salt water in your mouth into this cloth, filter it through the cloth into another bowl, and use it to wash your eyes—both of them about fifteen times each. After that, you should wash your eyes and rinse your mouth with warm water from yet another bowl. With this, you are finished.

If you do this every morning without fail, your teeth will not become loose for a long time, and they will not fall out even as you get old. You will also have no cavities. Your eyes will remain clear as well, you will suffer no eye disease even as you reach old age. You should be able to read and write small characters even at night.

This is an excellent method for taking care of your eyes and teeth. There are many people who have tried it and found it to be efficacious. I myself have practiced it for a long time. The proof of its efficacy is that, at eighty-four years old, I can write and read small characters even at night; that I have hard teeth, none of which has fallen out; and that I am free of eye and tooth disease.

If you do this every morning, it will become a habit after a while and you will be able to perform it without difficulty. More than that, you will never have to use a toothpick to clean your teeth.

284

You should not rinse your mouth with hot water. This will damage your teeth.

The ancients declared that disease of the teeth come from generative heat rising from the stomach. Thus, every day, you should from time to time clack your teeth together thirty-six times as though you were shivering. By doing so, your teeth will become hard, you will have no cavities, and you will avoid tooth disease.

You should not eat brittle foods when you are young, relying on the fact that your teeth are hard. You should not do things like crack the stones of plums and the seeds of arbutus,[7] as in later years your teeth will fall out prematurely.

If you often write in small characters, you will damage your eyes and ears.

You should not dig too deeply into the roots of your teeth with a tooth-pick. Doing so is apt to loosen your teeth and cause them to move in your mouth.

In the *Ch'ien Chin Fang* it says, "Every time you finish a meal, you should rub your face and massage your stomach with your hands, and get your saliva flowing. You should also take a walk of several hundred paces. If you lie down after eating or drinking, you will invite a hundred diseases. If you lie down looking up at the ceiling after eating or drinking, it will obstruct your *ch'i*.

289

In the *I Shuo*[8] it says the following: "After eating, you should not go to sleep right away, even if you are tired. You should move your body a bit and walk quietly for two or three hundred paces. After doing this, you should unfasten your belt, loosen your clothing, and sit straight up, extending your back. You should then massage your chest and stomach with both hands, going back and forth across this area twenty times. This done, you should press and rub the area between your sides and hips in a downward motion twenty or thirty times. The *ch'i* in your chest and belly will thus not be obstructed and, with the motion of your hands, whatever remains in your stomach will be digested."

290

The eyes, nose, and mouth constitute the five apertures on the face and, being the locations where *ch'i* exits and enters, are the places from where it easily escapes. You should not allow *ch'i* to escape in great quantities. The urethra is a place from which the essential *ch'i* escapes, but this should not occur too often. The anus is the place from which excrement and *ch'i* exit the body, and you should not void excrement as a catharsis, with the resultant loss of *ch'i*. Generally speaking, all seven apertures should be tightly closed to prevent too much *ch'i* from leaking out.

291

A *kinro* is something constructed by putting a small scaffold over an open hearth, then placing a thick cloth over the scaffold in a tent-like fashion to trap the heat of the hearth and warm the body. Maintain a low fire in the hearth. This is commonly called a *kotatsu*.[9] If you warm your body too much, your *ch'i* will slacken and rise, your body will become lax, and you may suffer problems with your eyes. Only those beyond middle age should keep a warm fire under the *kotatsu* to avoid the cold. You should not sit on your behind and stick out your feet under a *kotatsu*, and a young person should not use one at all. During times of intense cold, a young person should sit by a hearth or make an open-air fire. You should not warm your body too much.

Evacuation of Bladder and Bowels

292

When you have an empty stomach, you should sit down to urinate. When your stomach is full, you should stand to urinate.

293

The evacuation of bladder and bowels should be performed and finished quickly. It is harmful to repress these urges. You may unexpectedly become busy and not have the time to evacuate your bowels or bladder. But if you repress the urge to urinate for a long time, you may momentarily block your urine and bring on an ailment that prevents its passage. This is called "anuria" or "dribbling."

If you repress the urge to evacuate your bowels often, you may contract hemorrhoids. Also, you should not strain too much when evacuating the bowels. This may cause your *ch'i* to rise, be harmful to your eyes, or cause heart palpitations. This can be very harmful. It is best to let Nature take its course.

It is beneficial to take a medicine that will stimulate your saliva, keep your body lubricated, and circulate the *ch'i* of your stomach and intestines.

Or you may eat things like hemp seeds, sesame seeds, and the kernels of apricots and plums. Constipating foods like rice cakes, persimmons, and mustard should not be eaten when you are constipated.

Constipation itself is not harmful, but not being able to urinate for a long time is dangerous.

294

People who are constantly constipated should visit the bathroom every day and pass whatever they can, even if just a little, without making too much of an effort. If they can do this, they will not be constipated for long.

295

You must not evacuate either bladder or bowels while facing the sun, moon, heavenly bodies, North Pole, or a Shinto shrine. Neither should you urinate on the ground on which the sun or moon is shining. Generally speaking, you should have great respect for the gods of Heaven, the gods of Earth, and people's souls. You should not make light of these things.

Bathing

296

You should not bathe too often. Too much warmth will open up the pores of the skin, and your *ch'i* will decrease as sweat is released. The ancients bathed once every ten days. This is certainly understandable!

You should bathe from time to time in a deep tub in which a little bit of warm water has been placed. Your *ch'i* will not decrease if the water is shallow and not overly heated. If the tub is deep, you will not be exposed to cold winds. But you should not bathe in deep warm water for a long time and overheat your body. When your body is hot, your *ch'i* rises, sweat is released, and your *ch'i* decreases. This can be extremely harmful.

You should not pour a lot of extremely hot water over your shoulders and back.

297

Bathing in hot water is harmful. You should test the degree of acceptable heat or cold for yourself. You should not bathe in hot water just because it feels good. Your *ch'i* will rise and decrease. Particularly, people with eye problems and those who have become chilled should not bathe in hot water.

298

Other than during the hot months, you should wash your hair once every five days, and bathe once every ten. This is an ancient rule. You should not bathe often except during the summer months. Though it may make you feel good, your *ch'i* will decrease.

299

Put a little warm water in a tub, pour some more warm water over your shoulders and back, and then finish up quickly. If you do this, your *ch'i* will circulate well and your food will be digested.

During the cold months, warm your body and improve your yang *ch'i*. You will not necessarily produce sweat. If you do this, you will not suffer harm even if you bathe frequently. When you do bathe frequently, just pour the warm water over your shoulders and back, but do not brusquely wash off the dirt. Simply, wash the lower part of your body and finish up quickly. You should not bathe too long and overheat your body.

300

You should not bathe on an empty stomach. You should not wash your hair when completely full.

301

Women should not wash their hair when their period has started.

302

When you have a small wound on your body, if you take a bath in hot water and then expose yourself to the wind upon getting out, the pores of your skin will close up and the heat from the bath will be sealed within you. Thus, even a small wound will turn in under your skin and produce a fever. This may halt urination and cause you to swell up. Such a condition is extremely dangerous, and for many it ends in death.

You should be very mindful not to expose yourself to the wind after bathing in hot water. It is commonly said that "hot water steams a small wound within." However, that is not it. When you bathe in hot water, the pores on the surface of your skin open up and become sensitive to the wind. With a cool breeze, they close up, sealing in the heat so that even a small wound is enclosed within.

After you take a bath, you should avoid exposure to the wind. If a wind comes up, you should quickly rub your skin with your hands.

There are hot springs in every province in Japan. Depending on the disease, bathing in them may have good, bad, or indifferent effects. These are generally the three conditions of which you should be mindful when you select a place to bathe.

Hot springs therapy is good for external ailments and is remarkably effective for complaints such as bruises, traumas received from falling off a horse or from a high place, skin ailments such as scabies, sword wounds, or ongoing boils. It is also good for paralysis, muscle cramps, withered limbs, numbness, or the loss of strength in the hands and feet.

Hot springs are not appropriate for internal ailments. Nevertheless, for complaints such as depression, lack of appetite, poorly circulating *ch'i* in the internal organs, disorder between blood and *ch'i*,[10] and general ailments that cause the body to feel cold, being warmed up by bathing in hot springs will be good for you by circulating your *ch'i*. But it will not produce the same quick results that it does on external ailments, and you should bathe with caution.

There are also many conditions in which bathing is neither beneficial nor harmful. In such cases, you are better off not bathing.

But in the case of certain ailments, bathing can cause great harm. These include profuse sweating, chronic exhaustion, and conditions involving fevers. For these, hot springs definitely should be avoided.

You should not go to a hot springs arbitrarily. There are many people who have taken hot springs therapy that is inappropriate to their condition, contracted yet another disease, and died. You should be mindful of this.

People make a great mistake when they do not understand the principles involved and believe that hot springs therapy is good for any disease. In this regard, the theories of Chen Tsang-chi[11] in his book *Pen*

Ts'ao should be reflected on, since he elucidates the facts on hot springs therapy.

Generally speaking, even a sick person who is constitutionally strong should enter the baths no more than three times a day. A weak person should bathe only once or twice a day. This, of course, will depend on the length of the day, but bathing often should be strictly avoided.

Even a strong person should not overheat his body while bathing. He should sit at the edge of the bath and pour warm water over himself with a ladle. He should not take a long time, but finish up quickly. He should not become overheated and start sweating. This should be strictly avoided.

During therapy you should take a light bath every day and finish quickly. The number of days of the treatment should be one or two weeks.

You should not drink the water of a hot springs, as it can be harmful. There are people who, in the treatment of sword wounds, have gone to a hot springs for a cure. While enjoying the efficacy of the water, they have drunk it, thinking that they would recover that much faster. However, their wounds were only exacerbated, and they died.

304

While you are taking hot springs therapy, you should not eat spicy food or any food that will raise your body temperature. Neither should you drink a lot of alcohol or eat large quantities of food. You should take a walk from time to time, move your body, and circulate your breath.

While taking hot springs therapy, you should avoid sexual intercourse assiduously. After you have left the baths, you should abstain for another ten days. You should also abstain from moxa treatment for the same period of time.

During hot springs therapy, and for at least ten days following, you should take supplementary medicines. During that time, you should eat good quality fish and poultry a little at a time. This will aid the efficacy of the medicines and will nourish your spleen and stomach. You should not eat raw or chilled foods, or foods of poor quality. Again, you should not drink large amounts of alcohol or eat large quantities of food.

It you do not take good care of yourself after a hot springs treatment, it will have no benefit whatsoever.

305

When drawing sea water for a bath, you should mix it with equal parts of either well water or river water, and then bathe. If you do not do this, it will bring on a fever.

306

People unable to go to hot springs will have the water brought in from afar. This is called "sympathetic bathing." If during the cold months the nature of this water is not damaged and you bathe in it, there may be some small benefit. However, there are people who say that the *ch'i* of the hot water that bubbles up from the ground of a hot springs is lost in the transportation process, and that the yang *ch'i* dies out altogether. Thus, they say, the water goes bad and is inferior in quality to pure water that has just been drawn.

Disease, Your Doctor, and the Art of Medicine

Illness is a great matter for one's person,
as upon it hangs life and death. It is not unreasonable
that the sages were extremely mindful of this.

Being Mindful of Disease

307

An ancient saying has it that you should "Always keep disease in mind." That is, when you are not ill, you should imagine the vexation of the days when you were ill. If you ward off the negative external influences, control your internal desires, are mindful of your mobile and resting periods, you will not get sick.

Another saying suggests that "When you are idle, always think about the times you were painfully ill." In other words, when you are relaxed and in good health, take the time to recall the anguished moments of past illnesses. A dose of preventative thought works well and is much more desirable than dealing with the consequences once you have taken ill.

The lines in a poem by Shao K'ang-chieh[1] echo these sayings:

Taking good medicine once you've become ill,
Does not equal taking care of yourself beforehand.

308

If you are mindful while in good health, you will avoid illness. Once ill, even with medicine your recovery will be difficult and slow. Be mindful of even the smallest desire or you could become gravely ill. Being mindful of small desires is easy when you remember that the vexations of a grave illness are many. Think about the pain of illness beforehand and have great respect for the disasters that can come afterward.

309

Another of the ancient sayings states that "Slight recovery aggravates an illness." Many people become lackadaisical and unmindful as soon as they are feeling slightly better even though they have yet to fully recover. This can lead to a relapse. When you have recovered a bit, try to become more mindful. If you avoid negligence, you should recover quickly and will prevent the disaster of recurrence. If you are not firmly mindful at this stage, you will gain nothing, even with repentance.

310

In the *Ch'ien Chin Fang* it says, "Do not be extreme in keeping yourself warm in winter or cool in summer. Generally speaking, a moment of extreme comfort will inevitably lead to disaster in the end."

311

When a person becomes ill, the mental distress and physical pain can be excruciating. The ordeal begins: calling a doctor, taking medicine, receiving treatments such as moxa or acupuncture, reducing your food intake, refraining from alcoholic drinks, troubling your mind in various ways, and putting up with the inconvenience and pain as all these treatments attack your body. However, if you just control your inner desires and protect yourself from negative exterior influences, you can avoid disease and all the ramifications.

Being patient and mindful at the beginning may be slightly troublesome, but it will have the great benefit of alleviating distress. Following such a path has the additional benefit of allowing you to avoid all the undesirable treatments and pain associated with illness.

An ancient saying tells us that "To be mindful of the end, be mindful at the beginning." The Way of Nurturing Life follows this in particular.

312

If you are firmly mindful and are reasonable with your inner desires for drink, food, and sex, and if you carefully guard yourself from the harmful external influences of wind, cold, heat, and humidity, you will avoid sickness, though you take no medicine. You will not become vexed.

If you give in to your desires recklessly, you may try to counter this by taking medicinal aids and relying on diets, but these measures are likely to have little effect.

313

A sick person mindful of the Way of Nurturing Life should not be pained or vexed during his illness. To become vexed blocks your *ch'i* and exacerbates your illness.

Even a severe illness, if properly attended to, will be easier to cure than you might think.

There is no benefit to worrying about an illness, but there is benefit to being mindful.

If your disease is fatal, there is no benefit to being vexed by what has been determined by the will of Heaven. To distress others about this is foolish.

314

Do not rush to cure an illness. You will only aggravate things. Making an unremitting effort to cure a disease is not to be equated with rushing.

While seeking to return to health, let Nature take its course in regard to the pace.

In all things, to do something too well will, on the contrary, only make it worse.

<h1 align="center">315</h1>

The rooms where we live and sleep should always be protected from the poisonous *ch'i* of wind, cold, heat, and humidity. Exposure to these elements can lead to an extraordinarily swift debilitation of the body. Humidity weakens the body slowly, but it does so profoundly. While people are usually apprehensive about the first three external influences, they do not fear the *ch'i* of moisture. Yet its effect can be severe and take a long time to remedy.

You should quickly leave such humid places as the banks of mountain streams. Further, you should not sit or lie down on shallow soil, in proximity to water, or on an unelevated floor. If the floor is elevated with open apertures or spaces beneath it, *ch'i* should pass through harmlessly.

You should not sit or lie down near a wall that has been newly plastered. This will expose you to humidity, making you ill with something difficult to cure.

A sickness brought on by humidity could cause an epidemic. This warning is not to be taken lightly. During the Korean campaign in the Buntoku era (1592–96), the deaths in battle were few, but those from epidemics were many. The encampments were in low areas and the soldiers were exposed to cold and moisture.

The places where you sit and the rooms where you sleep should be elevated substantially above moist ground. This will protect you from external humidity. Once exposed, you will find the effects difficult to cure. You should respect this fact.

To protect yourself from internal humidity, you should not drink too much alcohol, tea, or warm water, nor eat too many melons, too much fruit, or a lot of cold noodles. If, during the summer months, you drink too much cold water or consume too many cold noodles, you are sure to be stricken by internal humidity and be troubled by *tangyaku*[2] and diarrhea. You must be mindful of this.

316

Palsy is not a disease contracted from exposure to external winds. Rather, it is caused by winds produced within.

When people who are fat and pale and who possess only a little *ch'i* pass the age of forty, and what *ch'i* they have declines, then they may contract this disease if they are troubled by the seven emotions and worn out by food and drink. Constantly consuming too much alcohol, they injure their stomachs and intestines, decrease their fundamental *ch'i*, and generate an internal fever. Because of this, a wind is produced within and their hands and feet shake. They become numb and weak and cannot function as they should. Their mouth becomes distorted and they are unable to speak.

All of this occurs because of an insufficiency of fundamental *ch'i*. Thus, this disease does not occur with those who are young and have strong *ch'i*. In the rare instance when it does appear, the youth will be fat and lacking in *ch'i*.

Drinking too much, drying out and heating up internally, and producing an internal wind is very similar to the severe lingering heat during the seventh and eighth months when the rain has not fallen for some time, the Earth's *ch'i* does not cool down, and the wind picks up.

This disease rarely occurs among teetotalers. If it does, they are either fat or lacking in *ch'i*.

When a person's hands and feet weaken, become numb, and lose sensation, he can be likened to a rotten tree that has lost its true integrity.

This indicates an insufficiency of *ch'i*, blood, and strength and involves a numbness and inability to move.

Fat and pale people should all be mindful of this beforehand.

317

Yang *ch'i* is engendered in the spring, and our skin, which has been closed up during the winter, softens as the surface *ch'i* gradually opens up. Nevertheless, the year's remaining cold is still intense and exposure to the wind's chill is still dangerous. You should be mindful of this. If you protect yourself, you should not experience the discomfort of colds or coughs.

Even the growth of the grasses and trees is easily damaged by the lingering cold. This being so, people, too, should have great respect for this period of coldness. Thus, according to the moment, you should exercise, aid the circulation of the yang *ch'i*, and encourage its generation.

318

In the summer, *ch'i* becomes more and more energetic, sweat leaves the body, and the pores of our skin open to a great degree. At this time, the harmful external influences have easy entrance.

You should not expose yourself to cool winds for a lengthy period of time, especially after a bath. Moreover, because the yin element retreats during the summer and the yin *ch'i* hides in the stomach, digestion slows down. Thus, you should not eat or drink excessively during this time. Eating heated food warms the spleen and the stomach. Avoid cold water and all raw and cold foods. You should not eat a lot of cold noodles. Weak people should be especially apprehensive about the distress of diarrhea.

Do not bathe in cold water. Even during severe heat, if you wash your face with cold water, you may injure your eyes. Neither should you wash your hands and feet with cold water.

Do not allow yourself to be fanned while asleep. Neither should you be exposed to a breeze while lying down. Avoid sleeping or sitting outside at night and exposing yourself to the *ch'i* of the dew.

Even during times of extreme heat, you should not cool yourself off. Neither should you rest on anything that has been heated by the sun for a long time.

319

The fourth month[3] is the month of pure yang. It is the time when sexual intercourse should be strictly prohibited. Also during this time, you should not eat pheasant, chicken, or any warm or heated food.

320

Of the four seasons, the summer is the time when we should protect and take care of ourselves the most. Cholera, sunstroke, overeating, general diarrhea, and diarrhea accompanied by fever are all easily contracted. You should prohibit yourself from eating raw or cold foods, and you should be mindful and take good care of yourself.

If the above diseases occur during the summer, your fundamental *ch'i* will decrease and you will experience extreme discomfort.

321

During the intense heat of the sixth and seventh months, your fundamental *ch'i* is liable to decline more than during times of intense cold, so you should take especially good care of yourself. This is the one time of the year when you should take medicine to help support your health.

322

During the summer months you should not let people go into old wells or deep holes in order to cool off. Such places are full of poisonous *ch'i*. As for old wells, you should first drop a chicken feather from above. If the feather does not descend smoothly, it indicates the presence of poison, and no one should be allowed entrance. If you light a fire and lower it into the well, then people may follow. Also, you may climb down a well after dropping a good bit of heated vinegar down the shaft.

At the height of summer, you should clean out your well and remove all the old water.

323

During the summer the pores of the skin are open. As the season's heat lingers on and is still intense in the seventh and eighth months (the end of summer and the beginning of fall), the pores do not close quickly with the start of fall. Since the surface *ch'i* has not yet hardened, if your skin is exposed to the autumn wind, it is easily breached. You should be mindful of this and avoid overexposure to chilly winds.

After the lingering heat of autumn has departed, anyone who is ill should receive moxa treatment here and there on his body, and thus protect himself from colds. By doing so, he will aid the yang element and avoid the unpleasantness of too much phlegm and coughs.

324

Winter is the time when the yang *ch'i* of Heaven and Earth retreats and lies low, and when a person's blood and *ch'i* are repressed. This is a time to put the mind's *ch'i* at peace, make it content, and conserve yourself well. If you warm yourself excessively, you will excite your yang *ch'i* and it will escape. Do not allow your *ch'i* to rise.

It is good to warm your clothes a little, but avoid making them hot. For the same reason, you should not layer your clothes excessively or warm yourself too much in front of a fire. You should not bathe in hot water. And you should not sweat excessively by working too much, which will also allow your yang *ch'i* to escape.

325

The yang *ch'i* begins to manifest itself at the winter solstice. This smallest bit of yang *ch'i* must be protected; you must not be too active. If you do not have some official responsibility on this day, you should not go out. Also, you should avoid sexual intercourse five days before the solstice and ten days after. Moreover, you should go in for moxa treatment.

In the *Hsu Han Shu*[4] it says, "Changing the water in wells and so on at the summer solstice and changing the fire at the family hearth at the winter solstice is for ridding the home of contagious diseases."

326

You should not receive acupuncture or moxa treatment during the winter months unless you have come down with a sudden illness. You should especially avoid such treatments during the twelfth month.

327

You should avoid massage during the winter months. There is no harm in applying a gentle *doin* to yourself, but you should not apply it too vigorously.

328

On New Year's Eve you should dust off your ancestral shrine and sweep away the dust from inside the house, especially from the bedroom. In the evening you should light the lamps, keeping the house bright until morning, burn incense here and there, set off firecrackers in the oven, light a fire, and aid the generation of yang *ch'i*.

At this time, the family should gather around the hearth in full harmony, refraining from arguments, criticism, or anger with any member of the family. You should congratulate your mother, your father, and your seniors; drink spiced wine together with all the young and old, high and low in the house; and enjoy the congratulatory atmosphere. Everyone should stay up all night to send off the old year and welcome the new. This is called "watching over the year."

329

If you eat hot food and start to sweat, avoid exposure to the wind.

330

Generally speaking, you should avoid moxa treatment in places on the body where you have received injuries as a result of having fallen from high places or having been pinned under large stones or trees. If you do receive moxa treatment, the medicine you take will have no effect.

331

A person who has been wounded by a weapon and is bleeding profusely will suffer from thirst. Do not give him water, as this would be extraordinarily harmful. Nor should he be allowed to drink rice gruel, as this would cause his blood to gush out and prove fatal. Such things should be understood beforehand.

332

Cuts, contusions, and open wounds should not be exposed to the wind. Neither should they be cooled with a fan. This could result in stiffness or cramps, or possibly tetanus.

333

If you set out on a long journey on a winter morning, you should drink some wine to fortify yourself against the cold. If you are not a drinker of wine, you should drink rice gruel. You may eat ginger as well. Do not expose yourself to the cold on an empty stomach.

334

You should not travel far enveloped in mist. If it cannot be helped and you must be on your way, you should protect yourself with food and drink.

335

When you have been exposed to intense cold, you should not eat or drink anything hot right away. When you walk through snow and chill your feet excessively, you should not wash them in hot water nor immediately heat them up next to a fire.

There are many ailments that lead to sudden death. These include stroke, paralysis, gas, poisoning, heat prostration, being frozen, scalding, food poisoning, sunstroke, tetanus, laryngeal diphtheria, pulmonary edema, loss of blood, contusions, and infantile diphtheria.

Beyond these, there are five other kinds of sudden deaths, termed the Five Extinctions. These are 1) hanging oneself, 2) being crushed to death, 3) drowning, 4) dying from fright in one's sleep, and 5) dying in childbirth. These are all conditions involving a violent death.

In normal times, you should prepare yourself for such things by studying books concerning them or asking a good physician about appropriate treatments. If you are not prepared beforehand, you will not know what to do during an emergency.

Even if you see miraculous or strange things happen right before your eyes, they are not necessarily the works of gods or demons. There are diseases of the mind as well as those of the eyes. When people have such illnesses, they will see many things that do not actually exist. You should not believe in them and become confused.

Choosing a Good Doctor

The Way of Nurturing Life encompasses many ways to preserve your health. Among them are being mindful of disease and judiciously selecting a doctor. It would be dangerous to entrust the future of your father and mother—for whom there is no replacement—or your future to a mediocre doctor. To place your father, mother, or children into the hands of a physician whose level of skills is unknown to you would be unfilial and unloving.

Ch'eng-tzu said that you must know something about medicine if you are going to take care of your parents. This is reasonable. If you have some general idea about the art of medicine, you will comprehend a doctor's strong and weak points. You need not have a full knowledge of the field. For example, though you may not be a skilled painter and calligrapher, if you have learned something of the techniques of the brush, you can appreciate the good and bad points of such arts.

339

Medicine is the art of human-heartedness.[5] A physician should build the foundation of his practice on human-heartedness and love, both of which focus on helping others. His intentions should not focus on his own profit and welfare. As this is an art of aiding people—who have been given their birth and nourished by Heaven and Earth—and takes charge of their life and death, you could say that a doctor is one of "humanity's officials." This is an extremely important position.

In other arts, if a man is not skillful, he does no great damage to another's life. But a man's life and death depend on the skill or clumsiness of a doctor's art. With this in mind, choose a person who has great talent *and* a capacity for learning to be your doctor.

340

Generally speaking, a person who intends to become a doctor must first read the Confucian classics and have a thorough knowledge of what is written therein. Because the Way of Medicine is founded on the principles of yin and yang and the Five Elements,[6] it is made clear by the Confucian classics and the *I Ching*. If he does not have that knowledge, he will not have the capacity to read medical books and it will be difficult to learn the art of medicine.

Sun Sze-mo said, "For the most part, if you aspire to become a doctor, you must first have a thorough knowledge of the Confucian classics." He also said, "He who does not understand the *I Ching* cannot become a doctor." These are credible words.

To study any art, you should make scholarship your foundation. If you do not, your technique may be mature, but the principles behind them will remain murky and your art will remain at a low level. And though the damage you cause is legion, if you have no scholarship behind you, you will not understand your own mistakes.

341

A good doctor is one who understands the Confucian classics, has a detailed knowledge of medicine, is interested in its techniques, has become familiar with many diseases, and understands the changes those diseases entail.

If a person becomes a doctor but does not really enjoy the study of medicine, does not intend to follow its Way, does not read medical books, does not clearly think through the books he has read, is not conversant with their principles, is a stickler for old theories even though he continues to read, and does not understand the changes of the times, then he is really just a low-class laborer.

Among the common run of doctors there are many who are quite clever with words and say that the study of medicine and medical treatment are two different things. They state that medical science has no application in the actual treatment of disease, and thus disguise their lack of knowledge. Such men are familiar with human emotions and the ways of the world. They associate with and flatter the aristocratic and powerful, making empty names for themselves and happily basking in the attention of society.

Such men are known as "Doctors of Fortune" [7] and "Doctors of the Times." They know little of the Way of Medicine, but with the good fortune of the moment, they treat one or two men of wealth and standing and, quite by accident, get a reputation. This is the same as someone without virtue or talent becoming wealthy and noble simply by being in the right place at the right time.

Just because a doctor is currently in demand does not mean he is a good doctor.

The ancients said, "A doctor must have a mind." [8] This "mind" means one that is clear on detail and, possessing a thorough grasp of the Way of Medicine, can treat disease well.

If a man is going to become a doctor, he should be a gentleman [9] and not a man of little character. A gentleman doctor practices medicine for the sake of others. His sole purpose is to help people. The doctor of little character practices medicine for his own sake. His commitment is to his own profit and well-being.

345

As medicine is the art of aiding the sick and ailing, a doctor should do everything he can to treat a disease, regardless of the patient's status, wealth, or lack of either. If he is asked to visit a sick person's house, he should go quickly, without regard for the real estate value of the residence. And he should not be tardy. A person's life is his most important possession, so one should not treat a patient lightly. This is the task and duty of a doctor.

If his medical practice is currently in vogue, a doctor of little character will believe that he is quite above others and will make light of his patients of low social standing and income. This is a doctor who has lost his original purpose.[10]

346

A person with some leisure should set himself to the task—at least a little—of understanding the outline of medical practice. This will allow him to judge whether a doctor is skillful or clumsy, have some concept of the basic medical herbs, and know the healing or deleterious effects of certain foods and medicines.

By reading medical books, he will be able to prepare emergency medications for everyday use. Thus, he may be able to provide emergency treatment while the doctor has not yet arrived, or take care of minor ailments in a village where there is no doctor, or even treat someone or himself while on a journey. In short, he will be able to take care of himself and help others.

If you have no knowledge of medicine, you will not be able to tell a good doctor from a bad one, and you will simply consider a skillful doctor to be one who is popularly employed and those not in demand to be quacks. Note that in the *I Shuo* it says, "An excellent doctor will not be as successful as one simply popular at the time."

There are numerous examples of people who have been unable to tell the difference between skillful and unskillful practice, have entrusted the lives of their parents and themselves to an average practitioner, and have been given the wrong treatment and have died.

You should consider such things deeply.

347

A mediocre doctor dislikes medical study and so avoids it. He reads books written by famous contemporary doctors, memorizes the use of fourteen or fifteen concoctions, but knows nothing of the Way of Medicine. Nevertheless, if he becomes familiar with the sick and dying and treats everyday diseases, he will do better than the man who reads medical books but who has had little experience with the ill. This can be likened to ripe barnyard grass tasting better than unripe grain.

A shoddy doctor without adequate medical learning is apt to take the false symptom for true, a chill for a fever. By mistaking one for the other, he brings on numerous disasters in diagnosis not apparent to the untutored eye. There are fevers that resemble chills, and chills that resemble fevers. There are true symptoms that resemble false symptoms, and false symptoms that resemble the true. And there are internal wounds that quite clearly resemble external ailments.

There are many diseases with symptoms that mislead the unprepared doctor. There are also deep-rooted diseases, diseases that are hard to diagnose, and rare diseases with which doctors are not familiar. The treatment of such diseases is extraordinarily difficult.

348

The ancients said that "The poor die from the lack of a doctor, the foolish die from choosing a mediocre physician." This is pitiful.

349

Someone once said that "Being sick but receiving no treatment can be equated with the practice of mediocre medicine." You should truly understand how reasonable this is. And this being so, when sick, you should only take the medicine prescribed by an excellent doctor. You should not take medicine prescribed by mediocre and inferior doctors.

These days excellent doctors are hard to come by. Most doctors are mediocre or inferior.

350

It has been said that if you are not prescribed medicine, a physician is of no use at all. I answer that this is not so, because not all diseases can be cured. One case for not taking medicine is that of a disease for which diagnosis is difficult—when chills and fevers, true and false symptoms are confusing and doubtful, and one disease may seem like another.

Mild diseases that are easily treated may be attended by an inferior doctor.

351

When a medicine is effective, it is either because it was appropriately prescribed or because it hit the mark by chance.

It is an undeniable fact that a mediocre doctor often misses the mark. Thus, you should always use an appropriate medicine prescribed by a good doctor. Never rely on a mediocre doctor.

An appropriate prescription is like the arrow of a skillful archer who always hits the target. An accidentally successful prescription is like the arrow of an untrained archer who sends it up with a prayer and fortuitously strikes the target.

352

Among those who aspire to be doctors, there are many who envy the "Doctors of Fortune" who have had the luck of the moment and been employed by the rich and noble, who make no efforts in medical studies, who will only go in and out of the gates of the powerful, who flatter others and seek to be engaged by them, and who thus gain fame and fortune. This is the very reason the art of medicine is declining, with practitioners' skills waning and medicine practiced to a great degree by mediocre doctors.

Advice on Becoming a Doctor

353

If a person studying medicine comes to understand that he was not born with the right mentality or talent for such work, he should immediately abandon the field. A man without talent will not understand the Way of Medicine well. He will only make many mistakes and hurt those beloved of Heaven, and this is a grave crime. We should all have a deep respect for the Way of Heaven. There are many other professions from which a man can choose, and he should direct his efforts to one of those fields.

If a student of medicine only trifles with the art, he turns his back on the Way of Medicine and will damage others. Not only that, but he himself will be unhappy. If a man is muddled and does not understand this art, but rather fabricates things, makes a show of whatever talents he has, criticizes some doctors, and is obsequious to others in order to gain their favor, he is to be held in contempt.

In the *Li Chi*[11] it says that "A practice of medicine can be considered good if it has been in a family for three generations." If a doctor's descendants are born with an innate talent for medicine, it is right for the profession to be carried on generation after generation. But such a thing is rare. Regardless of whether the three generations consist of father, son, and grandchild, if there is a teacher followed by a succession of *apprentices* for three generations, the practice will be well understood. However, though a man may be the son of a doctor, if talent is lacking he should not follow a family profession with inexpert skill.

354

Someone said, "Becoming a gentleman doctor and practicing medicine in order to save lives is certainly how it should be. Now if wealthy and noble people like Chung-ching and Tung-yuan become doctors, do not work for their own benefit and well-being, but are simply single-minded in helping others, they will still have no fear of becoming destitute. However, if the son of a low-income household does not work for his own benefit and welfare, but practices solely for the sake of others, he will have a hard time avoiding the travails of hunger and cold."

To this I answer: Becoming a doctor for the sake of my own benefit and welfare would be like a poor and humble person serving his lord for the sake of a stipend. In truth, although he does this work for the benefit of a stipend, once serving his lord, he forgets about himself and does the job solely for the sake his liege. This is a matter of fidelity to principles, and a man will sacrifice his one life regardless of the size of his stipend. This is the Way of a retainer. If a retainer works hard for his lord, the latter will respond to this debt of gratitude, and the retainer will receive his stipend automatically without asking.

In like manner, once a man becomes a doctor, he should single-mindedly work to cure men's ills and put all his energies into helping them live. This is exactly like serving a lord by forgetting one's own self and striving single-mindedly with loyalty and righteousness. Once engaged, a good man should not weigh things out from the standpoint of his own benefit and welfare

If you do cure the sick and help the ailing, you will receive your own benefit and welfare naturally from these activities themselves, and this without seeking for them at all. Simply put, practice the art of medicine with single-mindedness and be not greedy in seeking your own benefit and profit.

355

When a doctor is at home, he should always read medical texts and submerge himself in the principles therein. Thus, when calling on the ill, he can take into consideration all the information on treating the disease in question and carefully determine the proper medicine.

Generally speaking, the practice of medicine requires the single-minded following of its Way. A doctor should not dally with other concerns. If a doctor takes a patient into his charge, then he should not be distracted by other matters. If he is not single-minded, his practice will remain unrefined.

356

If the child of either a samurai or a commoner shows talent in medicine while still young, he should read the Confucian classics early on and, thus empowered, become familiar with books on medicine. If he exerts himself as an apprentice to an excellent doctor for ten years, reads such books as *The Yellow Emperor's Classic on Medicine* and *Pen Ts'ao*,[12] and then studies by reading books written by famous doctors of former generations, he will eventually have an understanding of the Way of Medicine. He should then work diligently for another ten years, seeing patients and gaining experience by observing their symptoms over long periods of time, contemplating the treatment techniques of older Japanese doctors famous in recent times, remaining with the ill for long periods, and understanding what changes occur over time. He should also become increasingly familiar with techniques and how they are appropriate to regional differences in Japan.

If he will thus commit to the lengthy period of twenty years in both medical study and actual treatment, he will become a good doctor, his treatments will be beneficial, and he should be able to help many people.

Practicing like this, a doctor will gain fame completely on his own. He will be called in for consultation by noble warrior families and important people and will be warmly respected and trusted by samurai and commoner alike. Thus he will receive plentiful recompense and have more than he needs for his entire life.

If a young doctor truly makes great efforts in this way and becomes learned in earnest, name and fortune will come as easily as bending down and picking dust up off the road. This is an excellent plan for the hard-pressed sons of samurai and commoners to gain fame and fortune.

A man with such skills is a treasure to his province. Lords and nobility should cultivate such a man early on.

Meanwhile, a person who imitates the techniques of mediocre physicians and believes their foolish and vulgar sayings will become not much more than a bungler.[13] The result will be the same if he fails to immerse himself in medical studies, follows along after common teachers, does not read the Chinese books on medicine, has no understanding of the causes of diseases and their progressions, is not familiar with basic herbs, cannot understand the characteristics of medicines, is in the dark about medical techniques, peruses only two or three chapters of recently published books written by Japanese doctors, has memorized only a few medical properties, dresses elegantly and makes a display of his appearance and behavior, speaks cleverly about explanations and theories, preens himself in order to be welcomed by others, humbles himself but speaks on familiar terms with the wealthy and noble, tries to be in the right place at the right time, and envies the "Doctors of Fortune."

Such doctors will tell people that the scholastic study of medicine results in sloppy treatment, and they will criticize doctors of learning.

A doctor takes charge of the infinitely important lives of the people who receive the compassion of the Heavenly Way and are considered its children. The use of the mean and narrow techniques described above for the treatment of the limitless diseases in this world is hardly worth discussion.

357

The person who desires to become a doctor must first establish his aspirations, have in his heart of hearts the desire to help all people regardless of their status or wealth, and have the capacity to administer the correct treatment.

If a physician is absolutely clear about the Way of Medicine and has a detailed knowledge of the art, he will quite naturally be held in great regard by others and receive countless blessings, though he neither inflates his own reputation nor seeks society's approbation. But if he acts only in the interests of his own benefit and welfare, has no desire to help others, and loses the fundamental intention of this art of human-heartedness, he is not likely to have the divine blessing of the Way of Heaven.

358

A man cannot understand the art of medicine unless he reads widely and thinks over what he has read. If he has not established the principles of the art in detail, the Way will not be clear.

It is absolutely necessary to study medicine both in broad terms and in detail, and the man who chooses to study medicine must make this his great purpose from the very beginning.

Though breadth and detail are two different things, a doctor must be equipped with both. His intentions must be great and his mind aware of detail.

359

Concerning the recitation of poetry, Abbot Shinkei[14] said, "There are people who have read widely in poetry anthologies and have a great knowledge of the subject, yet they are poor poets."

The art of medicine is exactly the same. There are doctors who have read many books on medicine and yet are not skillful. This is because they have not really used their minds to pursue the Way of Medicine and have no detailed knowledge of the subject.

Nevertheless, no man can be skillful without reading medical texts. There are many Confucian scholars who have studied broadly and gained great knowledge and yet do not understand the Way. However, there is no one who has understood the Way who has not studied extensively.

360

A doctor should practice with human-heartedness. Though a disease be grave and a prescription of no use, if the patient's family begs for medicine, a doctor should send a large dose just to console them.

Not giving a patient medicine and thus giving him up for dead is heartless. If a doctor will not prescribe medicine, the patient will only be all the more discouraged. This is pitiful.

361

In the study of medicine, a doctor should inquire into ancient methods, study broadly, and think extensively over the practices of former times. But he should also consider the changes of recent times, measure people's physical strengths and weaknesses, understand the environmental conditions in Japan and the people's practices and dispositions, as well as think through the treatments practiced by famous doctors in our country both past and present. Only then should he initiate his own treatment.

A doctor will make few mistakes if he bases himself on the old and is well-informed about the new. Conforming to the new without understanding the old is like working away with a clumsy chisel when one needs a more delicate instrument. But to be concerned only with the old while not conforming to modern improvements is like being stuck in the mud. The mistakes are exactly the same.

You should not practice medicine if you do not understand ancient practices and are not clear about the modern. The sage[15] said, "A master is the man who warms up the old, but understands the new."[16] A master of medicine is exactly the same.

362

A doctor should not criticize a patient's previous physician, even if the latter's treatment and prescription were faulty. Criticizing another doctor and praising one's own art is the practice of a man of little character. It indicates a narrow mind. Neither is it the true purpose of the practice of medicine. People who hear such scornful talk will surely find it despicable.

363

The ancients' theories on medicinal herbs were divergent rather than unified. They had their differences and similarities. You should think through these different theories and only *then* choose what you will use.

Both medicines and foods are either efficacious or not, according to a person's constitution and disease. They cannot be determined to be universally good or bad.

364

Although there are many aspects to the art of medicine, there are three essentials. The first is theory regarding the nature of disease; the second is diagnosis of symptoms; and the third is the prescription of medicine. You should understand these well. It is said that you should also understand things like horoscopes and angiology, but these come after the three essentials.

Theory regarding the nature of disease is based on *The Yellow Emperor's Classic on Medicine*, and study of this book should be augmented by thinking through the medical theories of all the famous doctors.

For the diagnosis of symptoms one should think through the books on symptoms written by a number of different schools. The prescription of medicines should be based on the *Pen Ts'ao*[17] and a broad view of the many books on the subject.

If you do not have a detailed knowledge of the character and quality of herbs, it will be difficult to make up a prescription, and those you do make may be inappropriate for the disease. Further, if you do not understand the good and bad points of foods, you will make mistakes in taking care of the sick and well alike. If you do not have a detailed knowledge of the *Pen Ts'ao*, it will be difficult to understand the characters and qualities of medicines and foods.

Advice on the Art of Medicine

365

Japanese medicine is not up to the level of Chinese medicine because Japanese do not make the same efforts in scholarship as do the Chinese. Particularly in recent years, many books on medical treatment have been published in the Japanese written language instead of Chinese. Medical students dislike ancient studies, and as they find Chinese books difficult to read, they avoid them with distaste. Such students believe that reading books in the Japanese syllabary is sufficient for learning the Way of Medicine, and so do not study the true ancient Way. Thus, Japanese doctors have a muddled understanding of the Way of Medicine and lack the proper skills.

The long-ago invention of the Japanese written language has resulted in illiteracy in the world at large.

366

In the various arts and crafts, there are many things that are of no practical benefit in everyday life. This claim cannot be made about art of medicine. Though you are not a student of medicine, you should give it some study. Generally speaking, Confucian scholars are supposed to understand everything under Heaven. Thus, the ancients said that medicine was also one of their subjects.

367

The art of medicine is especially useful in our own self-maintenance, the support of our parents, and the welfare of others. Thus, it is far more beneficial than all the other arts put together. You should not be without an understanding of this.

However, a word of caution: if you are not a student of medicine and have not learned the art of medical treatment, you should not just take medicine as you like.

Chapter 7

The Use of Medicine

General Remarks

368

It is impossible for the human body to be completely free of illness throughout its lifetime. When you are sick, you call for the doctor and ask for treatment. There are, however, three kinds of doctors: the superior, the middle ranked, and the inferior.

The superior doctor understands the nature of diseases, their symptoms, and the medicines used to treat them. By knowing these three things, he treats the disease and his services are beyond reproach. As the ancients used to say, such men are truly treasures in our world, and their merits are only second to the great ministers of state.

An inferior doctor has made no attainments in these three areas. He passes out drugs arbitrarily and brings many people to grief.

There are also middle-ranked doctors. Though such men do not understand the nature of diseases, their symptoms, and the proper medicines as well as superior doctors, they do know that medicines all distort the body's *ch'i* and should not be used arbitrarily. Thus, they will not prescribe medicine inappropriate to a disease.

On Doctors and Their Treatments

369

In the *Ch'ien Han Shu*, Pan Ku states, "If you have a disease that defies treatment, always take the middle course of medicine." This means that though you may be sick, if the disease is not clearly understood, the symptoms not clearly discernible, and the medical treatment cannot be pinpointed, it is better to be cautious and not administer a prescription. Taking the cautious approach and not treating a disease is the middle road in the practice of medicine.

The inferior doctor dispenses medicine at random and often brings people to pain and grief. Thus, when you are ill, if a good doctor is not available, avoid taking medicine prescribed by an inferior physician, who is little better than a quack, or you will bring harm to your body. If a good doctor is not on hand, you should simply be cautious, take good care of yourself, use no medicine, and wait for the disease to dissipate on its own. There are a number of diseases that—if you approach them like this—will go away on their own, without exposing yourself to either medicine or toxin.

The middle-ranked doctor does not come up to the standards of a superior doctor, but he considers his lack of knowledge to be exactly that, is cautious with the disease in question, and does not treat it indiscriminately. Thus the ancients famously said that being given no treatment despite being ill indicates a doctor of the middle rank.

The patient should also take this view to heart and not take any inappropriate medicines.

370

Now medicine is something that distorts both the good and bad *ch'i* that enters and leaves the body, causing chills and fevers. Because it is used to distort *ch'i* and thus attack the disease, even an excellent herb like ginseng should not be used irresponsibly.

A medicine may be considered good when appropriate to the disease, and there will always be some sign of this. A medicine may be considered toxic if not appropriate to the disease. Such medicines not only lack benefits but actually harm the patient.

371

There is an old saying that goes, "The injury from an illness can be cured, but the injury from medicine is quite difficult to treat." Thus, you should have great respect for medicine and take it cautiously. Even Confucius, when he was honored with a gift of medicine by Li K'ang-tzu,[1] said that he would not take it, claiming that as yet he was not familiar with it.[2] This is because he was very cautious about disease. We should take this great lesson from the sage as a rule.

372

Commonly, when someone contracts a disease, he seeks a hasty cure. Without distinguishing a good doctor from a bad one, he gulps down some quack's medicine and hurts himself further. Though you could say that such a person only seeks to nurture his health, in his haste he brings on only grief.

373

Nowadays, doctors pass out medicine without being clear about the origins of a disease, without looking into the symptoms in detail, and without understanding whether it will be appropriate to the disease. All medicines have a distorting toxin in them, and you should have great respect for this fact.

374

Sun Ssu-mo said, "People should not take medicine for no reason. If it only promotes distortion, your internal *ch'i* will lose its equilibrium and you will get sick."

375

Liu Chung-ta said in the *Hung Shu*, "If you are sick but don't have a smart doctor, do not take medicine. Just wait quietly for your condition to get better [on its own]. Do not love your body so much that you quickly consume medicine at random without discriminating between a doctor's good and bad points."

As medicines all have a distorting quality, if they are not appropriate to a disease they will certainly become toxic. For this reason, you should not take medicine indiscriminately for any disease.

376

There are more disasters resulting from medicines than there are from diseases. If you do not take medicine but are instead cautious and take good care of yourself, you will not be harmed by any drug and should recover quickly.

377

A good doctor gives medicine in response to the condition of the situation. He looks carefully at the circumstances of the patient's chills or fevers, checks true or false symptoms, responds to their momentary changes, and is in accord with what is right. This is not a matter of adhering to one absolute method. It is rather like a good general who fights his battles well by observing his enemies closely and responding to their changes. His methods are not determined beforehand. He observes the moment and is in accord with what is right.

A good doctor "warms up the old and understands the new."[3]

378

To nurture your spleen and stomach, it is beneficial to eat grains and meats. Medicines distort your *ch'i*. Though it might be said that ginseng and *jukkan*[4] are excellent medicines that have no toxins, we know that herbs with strong or violent stimulating properties can greatly decrease your fundamental *ch'i* if they are not appropriate for a disease.

For this reason, when you are not sick, you should simply nurture yourself with grains and meats. The good you will gain by doing so will far outweigh what you would gain from a supplement like ginseng. Thus the ancients said that supplementary medicine is not as good as supplementary food.

Old folks especially need some supplementary foods but should use supplementary medicines only when they absolutely must.

379

There are many diseases that will dissipate without the use of medicine. A person unaware of this fact may take medicine casually or indiscriminately and soon find that the medicine is attacking his body rather than providing beneficial effects. This could seriously aggravate the disease. Further, his food may be obstructed internally, his cure may be prolonged, and in many cases death may result. You should be very cautious with the use of medicine.

380

If the nature of a disease is not clearly understood at its outset, you should not immediately take medicine that *might* be beneficial. You should only use medicine *after* the nature of the disease is understood clearly.

The fact that various diseases can become extraordinarily grave is often due to *taking the wrong medicine at the outset*. If someone makes a mistake and uses medicine contraindicated by the symptoms, a cure will be difficult to attain. Thus the essentials of treatment must be established at the very onset of the disease.

That said, when you become sick, you should call a doctor quickly and be treated *for your condition*. Depending on the disease, if you are slow in its treatment, the disease may become grave and difficult to cure.

381

Ch'iu Ch'u-chi said that there is a Way to maintain health, but there is no medicine for a long life. In other words, there is a Way of Nurturing Life in yourself, but there is no miracle medicine that will extend the number of years you were born to live.

The Way of Nurturing Life is simply about taking care of yourself in order to maintain the number of years you were given by Nature. In ancient times there were many people who were deceived by magicians and took so-called life-extending herbs, but these had no positive effect. On the contrary, they sometimes brought people to grief because of their toxins. You should place no faith in such things.

If you control your internal desires, protect yourself from the negative external influences, are mindful of your daily activities, and move or rest at the appropriate times, you should be able to preserve the years given to you at birth. This is the Way of Nurturing Life.

Ch'iu Ch'u-tzu's assertion smashes the misguided ideas of antiquity, and you should align yourself with what he said.

By and large, doubt the doubtful and believe in the believable: this is the means of dissolving confusion.

382

At the pharmacy there are herbs and drugs both good and bad, real and fake, and you should be very careful in selecting them. Avoid those of bad quality or of questionable effectiveness.

You should also be cautious about the quality of each medicine. A drug may be perfectly prescribed for a certain disease, but if the quality is bad, it will not be effective.

It is also a good idea to be aware of how drugs are mixed. Though drugs may be of good quality, if they are used or mixed in unfortunate combinations, they may be ineffective or, worse, cause problems. Certain foods, for example, will taste good or bad according to the place and season. Similarly, good ingredients used by a bad cook will be tasteless and inedible.

Therefore, determine what drugs and herbs are of good quality, and ascertain the proper method for mixing them.

383

Supplemental herbs are apt to *not* pass through your system easily. If they remain in your body too long, they may be harmful or have no benefit at all.

Sustaining Old Age

384

As someone's child, you should not be ignorant of the Way of nurturing your parents. This is best accomplished by making their hearts glad, not going against their will, not making them angry, and not causing them anxiety. You should also make their bedroom and living room comfortable according to the heat and cold of the season, and make sure that their food and drink are tasty.

385

The physical *ch'i* of the elderly declines, and their stomachs and intestines become weak, so you must be careful with them just as you would be with a child. Ask after their likes and dislikes for food and drink, making sure that the temperature is neither too hot nor too cold, that their living room is nice and clean, and that they are well protected from the wind and rain. You should further see to it that they are warm in the winter, cool in the summer, well protected from the negative *ch'i* of wind, cold, heat, and humidity, that they are not upset by others, and that they always feel secure.

If there is some unforeseen disaster like a burglary, a flood, or fire, first make sure that your parents are not alarmed, then quickly escort them outside.

You should take great care that they neither meet with some untoward incident nor become ill. When the elderly become alarmed, they may become ill. You should keep this deep in mind.

Because they consider their remaining years to be few, the elderly are quite likely to have concerns that differ from those of their youth. It is more fitting that they should now have peace of mind, few affairs, and less social intercourse. This is included in the Way of nurturing the *ch'i* of the elderly.

When people get old, time goes by ten times faster than when they were young. They enjoy one day as if it was ten, ten days as if they were a hundred, and one month as if it were a year, so they should not lead futile lives. Every hour, every day should be valued.

You should nurture what physical health is left to them: their minds should be at peace, they should enjoy the days that remain in serenity, they should live without anger and with few desires.

For the elderly, one day spent without pleasure or in vain is a matter of deep regret. After a person gets old, one day is worth a thousand pieces of gold. As someone's child, shouldn't you keep this constantly in mind?

These days, many elderly people under the care of their children are apt to be angrier in their declining years than in their youth. They may also become avaricious, attack their children, find fault with others, and only demoralize themselves rather than hold firm to the integrity of their declining years.

How much better would it be if they spent their remaining years modestly, controlling their anger and desires, wearing their old age well, being patient in all things, not attacking the lack of filial piety in their children, and always enjoying themselves?

Confucius himself admonished us against the avarice that accompanies the decline of vigor in our old age, and we should have great respect for his words.

It is common for people to be quite modest when they are young. In old age, however, their desires proliferate, they are often angry and envious, and their declining years are lost to them. You should be mindful of this.

As your parents' child, you should think over these things and act so as not to incur your mother and father's anger. Think these things through ahead of time and be cautious. To make your parents angry shows a great lack of filial piety. Worse still is to anger your father and mother, and then to tell others that your parents have become senile. It is the practice of an evil man to be unfilial and then to resent his parents.

389

Taking care of the elderly involves placing great value on their fundamental *ch'i* and watching it constantly. It should not be allowed to decrease. Their breathing should be peaceful and not rough, their speech gentle and unhurried. Their words should be few, and their daily activities accomplished with composure.

Their speech should not be rough, fast, high-pitched, or loud. They should avoid anger and anxiety and should not linger on the past wrongs of others. Neither should they be overly regretful about their own past mistakes. Help them to be free from anger and spite over the impolite boisterousness of people at large.

All of the above are contained within the Way of Nurturing Life for the elderly. The elderly themselves should be mindful of this virtuous behavior.

390

Ch'i decreases naturally in old people, but this decrease should be prevented as much as possible. To avoid an excessive decrease of *ch'i*, the following activities should be avoided:

+ Most particularly, the elderly should not become angry.
+ They should be without resentment, sorrow, tears, and mourning.
+ They should not take part in funerals, or even make a sympathy visit to the family of the deceased.
+ They should not be made to think about things excessively.
+ Most importantly, they should avoid an excess of words. They should not discuss things in a quick manner.
+ Neither should they speak, laugh, or sing in a high-pitched voice.
+ They should not have to walk great distances down a road, or walk too fast.
+ Neither should they lift heavy things.

Especially in old age, *ch'i* should be valued.

391

The physical *ch'i* of the elderly is weak. It is important to keep it nurtured. In taking care of your parents, you should keep this fact in mind and not act negligently.

Most importantly, you should not go against your parents' wishes and should work to keep them happy. This will nurture their aspirations.

Also, you should not be negligent of their nutrition. You should offer them food and drink with a well-thought-out taste selection. Food that is not prepared thoughtfully or that is crude, bad-tasting, and of poor quality should not be offered because the elderly have weak stomachs and their intestines are easily damaged by rough fare.

People who are old and worn out have weak spleens and stomachs. It is most important to be cautious and protective of them during the summer months. If they eat raw or chilled foods because of the heat, they may be apt to get diarrhea. Fever and diarrhea are greatly to be feared. Once ill, such people can be worn down quite easily and lose even more of their fundamental *ch'i*. The remaining heat of the summer is particularly troubling.

During the cold months, the yang *ch'i* of the elderly decreases, and they are easily hurt by chills. One should be careful and protect them from such things.

393

Old people should avoid the following edibles in particular:

- raw and chilled foods
- tough foods
- burned or dried foods
- foods that are not fresh
- foods that smell bad
- oily or sticky foods that are not liable to pass through the system easily
- highly spiced foods, even if they taste good

In addition, special care should be taken about evening meals.

394

Being sad is unhealthy for an older person. Children of the elderly should visit with their parents from time to time, talk quietly about things past and present, and cheer them up.

395

Sometimes a person has good relationships with his friends, wife, and children and enjoys long conversations with them. At the same time, he considers his parents troublesome and keeps them at a distance. Such a person can be said to love others exclusive of his parents. This is called immorality and shows a lack of filial piety at its worst. It is also stupidity.

396

On days when the weather is warm and mild, you should take your elderly parents to a park, climb up to some elevated place, let them free their hearts from care, and relieve them of any depressing thoughts they may have. From time to time, it is good for them to refresh their minds by enjoying the outdoors and admiring the grasses and trees. The elderly should not have to trouble themselves by going out alone to parks or natural settings.

397

Due to their weak *ch'i*, the elderly should not overextend their vigor by ruminating on their past behavior, regardless of what may have occurred in the past.

398

When a person has passed his sixties and is into his seventies, just getting through a single year is a difficult matter. At this age, the loss of physical strength and *ch'i* in one year's time changes according to the season. This change is much more apparent than its passage over a number of years when one is young. Because of this steady physical decline, if an elderly person does not take care of himself, he will not be able to live a long life.

399

When a person reaches his seventies, one year goes by faster than did one or two months when he was young. With his days numbered and time passing so quickly, an elderly person will probably think about how many years he has left. It is foolishness for the child of such a person to fritter his time away without being single-mindedly filial.

400

After a person has reached old age, he should enjoy each day as though it were ten. He should not constantly begrudge the days or spend even one day uselessly. Even if the behavior of people in this world does not conform to his expectations, he should not consider others to be just common run-of-the-mill or unreasonable individuals. He should be lenient with the mistakes and bad points of his children and other people, and should not be a faultfinder.

The elderly should not be indignant or resentful. Even if a person is himself unlucky and poor, or treated shabbily by others, he should just consider this to be the way of this transient world, and neither turn his back on the will of Heaven nor give in to melancholy.

It is better to pass each day enjoying it. One should consider it regrettable to spend his days in pettiness by resenting others, being angry, troubling his own mind by lamenting his fate, and being generally unhappy. To spend even a single day in vain without enjoying that day, when time is to be so valued, is nothing but foolishness.

Even if your home is poor and unlucky and you eventually die of hunger, you should spend your time happily right up to the moment you expire. You should not—under the pretext of poverty—covet what others have and thus become an immoral person who regrets his fate.

As people get older, they should cut back on the number of their affairs, decreasing them as time goes on. They should not take pleasure in such things and avoid becoming increasingly involved in the world. When affairs are many, the mind is exhausted and happiness is lost.

When Chu Hsi[1] was sixty-eight, he gave his son a letter in which was written the following:

> Of the sick and worn out, many aggravated their illnesses by excessive eating and drinking. In particular, eating a lot of meat is harmful. Both morning and night, eat only one kind of meat and only a little of that. You should not eat a lot. If your soup contains meat, it is better that your side dishes do not. Evening meals without meat are the best. If your meats are varied and you eat one kind after another, they will not pass through your system easily and will cause you harm. Eating just a little bit of meat will 1) expand your stomach and nourish your *ch'i*, and 2) economize and save your assets.

Chu Hsi's words are pertinent to nurturing your health. Young people should act accordingly as well.

The elderly should not leave the house during strong winds or rain, intense cold or heat, or when the area is covered in a thick mist. At such times it is better to stay inside, avoid the exterior negative elements, and rest quietly.

404

When people get old, the *ch'i* of their spleens and stomachs declines and weakens, so it is better to eat less. Overeating is dangerous. Nine times out of ten, the sudden death of an elderly person is due to overeating.

Accustomed to having strong spleens and stomachs in their youth, the elderly eat too much, have indigestion, block their fundamental *ch'i*, and become sick and die. They should be mindful and not eat too much. Such foods as sticky rice, hard rice, rice cakes, dumplings, noodles, steamed rice with red beans, or red meat should be eaten only in small quantities, as they are difficult to digest.

405

The very first thing to be done when the elderly become ill is the regulation of their food. If the patient does not respond to a change in diet, then a regimen of medicine should be employed. This was the view of the ancients.

When the elderly are in good health, the benefit of nurturing them with grains and meats is far superior to such supplements as ginseng. For this reason, "supplemental nourishment" for the elderly should be employed bit by bit using tasty and quality foods.

406

When the elderly are not ill, they should not take medicine, which will only distort their system and cause them harm.

407

The elderly should eat only two meals a day, one in the morning and one at night. Only savory food should be offered. The elderly should not get used to eating in the afternoon, in the middle of the night, or at odd hours, as this may cause them harm. Especially when taking medicine, they should not eat at odd hours.

408

Once a person grows old, he should not scatter his mental faculties over all manner of things that do not give his mind pleasure. He should enjoy himself according to the moment.

Enjoying oneself in this instance means enjoying what will truly give him pleasure deep in his heart: not mulling over this anxiety or that, but taking pleasure in the four seasons, the scenery of the mountains and rivers, and the delightful proliferation of grasses and trees.

409

After getting old, a person who has no official responsibilities should constantly devote himself to nurturing both body and mind. He should not expend the vigor of his *ch'i* on activities unbeneficial to advanced age, as in the arts, which will only tire his mind.

410

In the morning, an elderly person should sit comfortably in a peaceful room, light incense, read or chant the classics of the sages and saints, cleanse his mind, and extinguish all thoughts of the vulgar world.

If the paths are dry and the wind is down, he should go out into the garden, take a relaxing and serene walk, and while admiring the grasses and trees, appreciate the scenery of the seasons.

Even upon returning to his room, he should enjoy himself as a man of leisure. From time to time, he should dust off his desk and inkstone and sweep away the dust from his seat and the first floor of his house.

He should not frequently stretch his legs out and lie down and sleep. Again, he should not have broad dealings with the common world, as this is not good for the elderly.

411

The elderly should always rest peacefully and not take part in rough behavior. There are cases in which a little bit of strenuous labor led to a minor injury and exhaustion and then, due to the ensuing anxiety, a quick and grave illness and death. The elderly should always be cautious.

412

The elderly should always sit cross-legged rather than with their lower legs tucked underneath them, reclining against something to support their backs. They should not get used to lying down on their sides.

Raising Children

413

The ancients said, "When raising a child, that child should know one-third of hunger and one-third of cold." This means that a child should have some experience of an empty stomach and some experience of the cold. This is good for adults as well.

It is a great disaster to feed children delicious foods until their stomachs are full, or to make them wear heavy clothing so that they are overly warm. The common man and his wife know little of scientific principles and so do not understand the Way of bringing up a child. It is a fact that feeding little children an abundance of delicious foods and clothing them so they are too warm will make them sickly and shorten their lives.

The children of poor families have limited food and clothing. Because of this they are healthy and long-lived.

414

A child's stomach and spleen are narrow and weak and thus easily damaged by food. You should constantly take care of him as you would a sick person.

A child has a vigorous yang element and so has many fevers. You should be constantly vigilant about this and work to reduce a fever as soon as it appears. If a child becomes too warm, his sinews and bones will become weak.

You should take a child outside when the weather is good and refresh him with the breeze and sun. If you follow this practice, his body will be strong and without disease. The clothing touching a child's skin should be made of old cloth. You should not use new cloth or cotton because it is too warm.

Postscript

I have recorded the words of the ancients in simple language and expanded on what they meant. There are also many things here that I have heard from my predecessors. I have further written down those things that I have tried myself and found to be efficacious, even though they might be thought of as conjecture. All of these things include only the gist of the Way of Nurturing Life. There would be no end to it if I recorded every last detail.

A person who intends to follow this Way of Nurturing Life would do well to read many of the books by the ancients and study them thoroughly. An understanding of the general outline will not allow you to follow the Way.

When I was young and reading through these many books, I collected the ancient sayings that expounded on the art of nurturing one's health, imparted them to those who had come to me to study, and had them classified in a book call the *Isei Shuyo* (1682). The person interested in the Way of Nurturing Life should also refer to this book. What I have written here is taken from the essentials of that book.

Written by an old man at the age of eighty-four
New Year's, 1713, an auspicious day

Kaibara Ekiken[1]

CHRONOLOGY
of Approximate Chinese Dynastic Periods

DYNASTIC PERIOD	YEARS
LEGENDARY SAGE EMPERORS	2852–2255 B.C.
HSIA	2205–1766
SHANG	1766–1045
CHOU	1045–256
WESTERN CHOU	1045–770
EASTERN CHOU	770–256
SPRING AND AUTUMN	722–481
WARRING STATES	403–221
CH'IN	221–206
FORMER HAN	206 B.C.–8 A.D.
LATER HAN	23–220
SIX DYNASTIES	222–589
THREE KINGDOMS	220–280
EASTERN TSIN	317–419
FORMER CH'IN	351–384
SUI	589–618
T'ANG	618–907
FIVE DYNASTIES	907–959
SUNG	960–1126
SOUTHERN SUNG	1127–1279
YUAN (MONGOL)	1279–1368
MING	1368–1644
CH'ING (MANCHU)	1644–1911

NOTES

INTRODUCTION

1 Pai-hun Wu-jen: An interesting name, literally meaning "master darkness no-man."

2 射 is both a noun meaning "archery" and a verb meaning "to shoot."

3 The man who has fully mastered the Way.

4 The Yellow Springs: Hades.

5 *Lieh Tzu*: One of the great books of Taoism, written, according to some scholars, around 300 B.C. The book is named after the Taoist philosopher who supposedly could ride the wind and lived around the year 600 B.C. It is a collection of sayings, stories, and short essays, and ranks third in importance in the Taoist canon, after the *Tao Te Ching* and the *Chuang Tzu*.

6 Cheng I-ch'uan (1033–1107). Early Neo-Confucian writer. Chan, page 552.

7 *Genki* (元気): Fundamental *ch'i*. This is the fundamental or primordial health with which we are endowed at birth, not simply the "health" or "vitality" conveyed in modern Japanese.

8 *Jen*, or human-heartedness, has been translated variously as virtue, compassion, love, or altruism. To Confucius, it was the basis of all goodness; to Mencius, it was natural to the human being, not something acquired by education. The character for *jen* (仁) is composed of two radicals (the one at the left for "man," the other for "two") that together signify society and, by extension, how we should act in society. With the *Yojokun*, Ekiken seemed to interpret the term with the Neo-Confucian understanding of "impartiality." Though he was born into a samurai family, he had much contact with people in the lower echelons of society, and the simple writing style of his book—uncommon for scholars of his day—would indicate that it was meant to be read by one and all, regardless of class.

9 "The Ten Thousand Things in Heaven and Earth" is an old Chinese phrase used in both Taoism and Confucianism meaning "everything in the world; all things in Nature; all things in the universe." Also, simply, the Ten Thousand Things.

10 This is the Great Way referred to by both Confucianism and Taoism. It is the Tao, the Way of the Universe with which both philosophies insist that we must be in harmony. The Tao is beyond definition. The very first line of the *Tao Te Ching* says, "The Way that can be intellectually understood [or defined] is not the everlasting Way."

11 See Note at the end of Preface.

12 Object: Literally, from the Japanese, a pot, vessel, or utensil; something that has function and can be used. In this case, probably anything in the universe that has form.

13 Sun Tzu (5th century B.C.) was a strategist and writer of the book that bears his name and is often entitled *The Art of War*.

14 In other works, Ekiken develops the theme of respect and gratitude toward Nature nearly to the level of modern-day environmentalism. Harming Nature and its creatures, he believes, is akin to parricide or matricide, and an act of extreme ingratitude and ignorance. It is like cutting down the stage upon which one acts.

15 A Japanese friend of mine recently informed me that the book had held an honored place on his father's tiny bookshelf and was referred to over and over, especially during the years of insufficiency following World War II.

16 Ekiken's ancestors had been priests at the Kibitsu Shrine near Okayama, which was dedicated to Kibitsu Hiko no Mikoto, the deified son of Emperor Korei (c. 215 B.C.). The shrine was built in the late fourteenth century, and Ekiken's ancestors were apparently its hereditary priests.

CHAPTER 1—The Way of Nurturing Life

1 The *Book of Documents* (書経): One of the five classics of Chinese literature, namely, the *I Ching*, the *Book of Documents*, the *Book of Rites*, the *Book of Odes*, and the *Spring and Autumn Annals*. The Five Happinesses are listed as longevity, wealth, health, love of virtue, and a crowning death.

2 The phrase "Ten Thousand Happinesses" is common parlance for all the happiness one can get out of life and, specifically, good health. It is not a philosophical term as is "The Five Happinesses."

3 Mind (心): In Chinese and Japanese, there is no differentiation between heart and mind. The reader is encouraged to recall this whenever either of these English words appears.

4 Yen Tzu: Confucius's favorite disciple, he died at a very young age.

5 See Introduction, Note 9.

6 Common decency. I take this reading of 礼, which is often translated as "rites," from Simon Leyes's *The Analects of Confucius* (W.W. Norton & Company, 1997, New York). Elsewhere, I have translated it as "proper manners," according to context.

7 Respect, Japanese *osore* (畏): The character is also read "*kashikomaru*," and means to sit straight or, rather, respectfully. Other common meanings are fear, reverence,

seriousness, and awe. In the Sino-Japanese lexicon, there are some thirty-five characters pronounced *"osore"* each with a slightly different nuance. The context suggests "respect" in the same sense that you might have "respect" for a rattlesnake in your path or a downed electric line after a hurricane.

8 Chu Hsi (1130–1200). One of the greatest Confucian scholars of China. His influence on Confucian thought in Japan was enormous, particularly during the Edo period (1600–1868), in which Kaibara Ekiken lived.

9 *Ninjin*: ginseng; *ougi*: a species of pea native to China, used as a stomach medicine and to stop night sweats and diarrhea; *byakujutsu*: a species of chrysanthemum (*Atractylodes japonica*) said to be generally good for the health and often taken at the beginning of a new year; *kanzo*: a species of pea native to China, used against coughs and stomach pain.

10 The educated or true gentleman, *kunshi* (君子), is the Confucian ideal of the man who is educated in both the literary and martial arts, and who understands and acts on the principles of humanity, loyalty, righteousness, and so on. This ideal was taken to heart by the warrior class in Japan, especially during Ekiken's time.

11 Poetry recitation and dance: The poetry recitation would have included traditional Chinese and Japanese poetry and the recitation of Noh librettos. The dance was probably specific to Noh.

12 See Note 7.

13 See Introduction, Note 10.

14 Shao Yao-fu, also known as Shao Yung (1011–77). A Chinese Neo-Confucianist much influenced by Taoism.

15 For Shao, Heaven and Earth are created and destroyed in cycles, the length of each being 129,600 years. See *A Source Book in Chinese Philosophy* by Wing-tsit Chan, page 487.

16 Spirit (霊): Ekiken repeats this phrase often in his writings.

17 The four classes of people were: farmers, samurai, artisans, and merchants.

18 Amaterasu-o-mikami: The Sun Goddess and ancestor of the Japanese imperial family.

19 *Nihon Shoki*, or *Nihongi*: The second-oldest written history of Japan, completed around 720 A.D.

20 See Note 10.

21 The kanji 酒, read either *sake* or *shu* in Japanese, shows the water radical next to a jar and indicates a fermented or alcoholic drink. In early Chinese history, this probably referred to a fermented drink made from millet or barley in the north, and later to one made from rice in the south. Fermented rice sake seems to have been brewed in Japan following the introduction of rice culture during

the third century B.C. It has been steadily refined since the eighth century A.D.

The term "sake" in Japan can be used broadly for alcoholic drinks in general, but it is also commonly used to indicate what is called "rice wine" in English. The term "*nihonshu*, or" "Japanese sake," is used to indicate "rice wine" to the exclusion of all other alcoholic drinks.

Ekiken seemed to refer to "rice wine" when using the word "sake", and he definitely differentiated it from *shochu*, a lower-grade alcoholic drink brewed from potatoes, millet, or barley. Interestingly, the rice wine of his time was of the *nigori* type, a sake filtered through a course mesh that left rice solids in the finished product. He also writes about sake from Europe, by which he means wine made from grapes, and at times alcoholic drinks from China. Since Ekiken's observations most often apply to the wider category of alcoholic drinks, we use the word "wine" for sake unless otherwise indicated.

22 "Autumn hair" (秋毫) in Oriental literature usually indicates something thin and insignificant. It refers to the fine, downy hair that grows on wild animals in the fall and helps keep them warm during the winter.

23 Po Chu-i (772–846): A T'ang-dynasty poet widely read in Japan.

24 See Note 3.

25 Tu Mu (803–52): A Chinese poet of the T'ang dynasty.

26 See Introduction, Note 13.

27 See Note 7.

28 Sun Chen-jen: A T'ang-dynasty doctor.

29 Hua T'o: A famous doctor of the Wei dynasty (220–64).

30 *Lu Shih Ch'un Ch'iu*: A philosophical book including Taoist and Confucian thoughts and sayings as well as a synthesis of philosophical theories and common knowledge of the times. Presented in twenty-six chapters by Lu Pu-wei (died c. 235 B.C.).

31 An abbreviation of the *Fei Chi Ch'ien Chin Yao Fang*, a medical encyclopedia compiled by Sun Chen-ren.

32 Supplementary medicines: Vitamin supplements and health drinks.

33 "Pure *ch'i*" refers variously to the *ch'i* that is the foundation of Heaven and Earth and the Ten Thousand Things, as well as to the soul, and, in Taoist health literature, to sperm and the corresponding fluid in women.

34 Keeps his mind clean (腹中を清虚にす): This phrase also possibly could mean "keep your intestines clean," or "keep your temper even."

35 Patience (忍): Can also be read to mean "endurance."

36 Wu Wang (武王): A first-generation king of the Chou dynasty; considered a great and wise ruler.

37 *Shang Shu* (尚書): One of the "Five Classics" of Chinese literature; also called

the *Shu Ching* (書経). In English the name is rendered as the *Book of Documents* or the *Book of History*.

38 In Chinese and Japanese medicine, the stomach is considered equivalent to the element earth, and the very center of the Five Elements: wood, fire, earth, metal, and water. They correspond to the Five Organs, namely, the heart, liver, stomach, lungs, and kidneys, respectively.

39 This seems to be a pulse we can feel. Doctors of Oriental medicine take the pulse by placing three fingers on the radial artery of each forearm. By exerting various degrees of pressure, they can understand the conditions of the body's internal organs (on the left, the small intestine, heart, gall bladder, liver, bladder, and kidneys; on the right, the large intestine, lungs, stomach, and spleen). Ekiken does not specify what pulse he is taking.

40 Chuang Tzu: An early Taoist philosopher and author of the book that bears his name.

41 Principle (理): It does not mean moral principle but, rather, natural law, the way things work, or the principles of the universe. Martial artists must understand principle in order to develop a true grasp of techniques; doctors must understand the principle of things in order to understand the nature of disease and how to deal with it.

42 Heaven's command (天命): Initially understood as the commands of a supreme anthropomorphic God, but later considered to be the Tao or its moral order. In the *Doctrine of the Mean*, it says: "Heaven's command is called human nature. To follow our nature is called the Way." Thus, an individual's natural endowments, his strengths and weaknesses, are considered to be the command given to him by Heaven.

43 The two types of massage are *doin* (導引), a Taoist technique introduced in Chapter 5, and *anma* (按魔), which seems to be the sort of massage generally in use by masseuses today.

44 The Chinese Methuselah. He is reputed to have lived during the Shang dynasty.

45 See Note 7.

46 See Note in the Preface.

47 Ill, Japanese, *byoki* (病気): The word literally means "afflicted *ch'i*."

48 Japanese, *tanden* (丹田): Literally, "the field of the pill of immortality."

49 The *tsun* is different for each individual. It is the distance between the top of the line beneath the first knuckle to the top of the line beneath the second knuckle on the bent index finger.

50 *Nan Ching*: A medical book compiled by a famous doctor, Ch'in Yueh-jen, during the Chou dynasty. Two chapters.

51 The Twelve Meridians: The energy ducts connecting the Five Organs (heart,

lungs, liver, kidneys, and spleen) and the Six Viscera (throat, stomach, large intestine, small intestine, gall bladder, and urinary bladder). When the five organs are considered alone, they are listed as in Note 38; when mentioned as the "Five Organs and the Six Viscera," they are listed as in Note 51. The difference, most likely, consists in their roles as tools of diagnosis and prescription.

52 In the Taoist practice with which Ekiken was probably familiar, this could be done sitting, standing, walking, or lying down.

53 Hips: In Taoist medical lore, this would be the sacrum. But, since Ekiken was writing for the nonspecialist, his term *koshi* (腰) probably referred to the hips or waist.

54 "Lightly," following the translation into modern Japanese by Maeda Michio. The term is 微気, which might also be translated as "rarefied or sublimated *ch'i*." Maeda suggests that here Ekiken could mean "abdominal breathing."

55 Decrease: The word is literally the adjective/adverb 少, meaning "a little." In this section, however, it is used as a verb, necessitating a minor change in the English translation.

56 Only eleven items appear in the text. In checking two additional sources, the same eleven appear. One editor noted that there may only have been eleven. Another possibility is that the discrepancy simply slipped by Ekiken and his publisher.

57 Sun's list differs slightly from that of Ekiken. Sun encourages us to decrease our yearnings, thoughts, desires, affairs, words, laughter, anxieties, pleasures, joys, anger, likes, and dislikes.

58 Blood vessels (血脈): Probably indicates blood pressure.

59 See Note 43.

60 神: Spirit or, perhaps, nerves.

61 精気: Essential *ch'i*.

62 *Shou Ch'in Yang Lao Shu*: A book authored by Liu Shun, who practiced medicine during the Ming dynasty.

63 T'ang Ch'un: A Ming-dynasty doctor.

64 生気, literally "life-*ch'i*": This is man's vitality, that which gives one animation.

65 The five watches of the night are: 7 p.m.–9 p.m., 9 p.m.–11 p.m., 11 p.m.–1 a.m., 1 a.m.–3 a.m., and 3 a.m.–5 a.m.

66 See Note 10.

67 *Way of Change*: The philosophy contained in the *I Ching* and its studies.

68 *Jio, chimo, obaku*: The herbs *Phellodendri cortex, Anemarrhenae rhizome*, and *Scrophulariae radix*, which are said to enrich the body's yin and to bring down the body's internal temperature.

69 *Ubu*: Also called "*torikabuto*," it is probably *Aconitum chinese*, which is said to replenish the body's yang.

70 Tan-ch'i: A doctor of the Yuan dynasty.

CHAPTER 2—Food, Drink, and Sexual Desire

1 Pure liquid (精液): The pure liquid that supports animal life. It later changes into blood and sperm.

2 Ekiken is referring to the *Analects*, 10.8:
[The sage] does not turn his back on high-quality rice or meat that is finely sliced. He does not eat food that has gone bad, fish that is not fresh, or meat that is spoiled. He does not eat food that has lost its color, that smells bad, or is improperly cooked. He does not eat food that is out of season, cut improperly, or prepared with an inappropriate sauce. Though there is plenty of meat, he does not take more [than his portion of] rice. He does not put limits on wine, however, so long as he does not get too tipsy. He does not drink wine or eat dried meat that is sold in shops. He does not exclude ginger from his meals, but does not eat a lot of it.

3 In the *T'sai Ken T'an*, written around 1600 in China but not printed in Japan until 1822, we read:

Strong wines and fatty meats, sweets and spicy foods—
These do not have true taste.
True taste is only in the light and simple.
The mysterious and strange, the preeminent and uncommon—
These are not men with true wisdom.
The man with true wisdom is only the ordinary man.

The Roots of Wisdom
Hung Ying-ming, page 25

The "light and simple" (淡): One of the core concepts of both Hung's and Ekiken's philosophies. It can be translated variously as light, simple, weak-flavored, or plain, as context dictates or as it is used in conjunction with other characteristics. Made up of the radicals for "fire" and "water," it would seem to mean washed out in color and taste. It is indicative of weak tea, thin wine, or a dinner of herbs, and this side of life is the core of existence. The opposite of this quality is the "thick and colorful" (濃), which may also be translated as the voluptuous and rich. It is used to describe bright colors and rich meats and has a connotation of the showy and gaudy. This quality is a distraction to real living and a detriment to true health.

4 See Chapter 1, Note 3.

5 Cowardice (臆病): Being fearful of disease. Or, the disease of fear.

6 The five grains: wheat, rice, beans, foxtail (German millet), and Chinese millet.

7 *Amazake*: Literally "sweet sake," it is a sweet drink made from fermented rice.

8 The Five Views (五観): Also referred to as the Five Meditations or Five Gazes, it refers to the description of the qualities of Kannon (Sanskrit, Avalokiteshvara) in the *Kannon Kyo*, the twenty-fifth chapter of the *Lotus Sutra*: the true view, the pure view, the view of great and encompassing wisdom, the view of pity, the view of compassion.

9 Li Li-weng: Also called Li Yu. An early Ch'ing-dynasty literatus.

10 Pure (清き物): This could be either "pure" or "clean."

11 Li Shih-chen: A doctor at the end of the Ming dynasty.

12 Su Tung-p'o: Also known as Su Shih (1037–1101), he is one of the greatest poets of the Sung dynasty.

13 The first day of spring: Around February 4 or 5.

14 Chang-lai: A poet of the Northern Sung dynasty.

15 *Ku Chin I T'ung*: A book written by a Ming-dynasty doctor, Hsu Ch'un-fu.

16 See Chapter 1, Note 21.

17 Shao Yao-fu (1011–1077): A scholar of the Northern Sung dynasty.

18 Po Chu-i (772–846): One of the greatest poets of the T'ang dynasty and of all time.

19 *Wu Hu Man Wen*: A book of essays from the Ming dynasty. Among the men mentioned are Chang-weng, aged 113; Wang Ying-chou, aged 130; and Mao Chien-weng, aged 103.

20 In Ekiken's time, *shochu* was a spirit most often made from potatoes but also from wheat and other foodstuffs. It was a unrefined drink with an alcohol content of twenty to twenty-five percent.

21 Satsuma and Hizen were both provinces on the southern island of Kyushu.

22 The word 国 can mean either "country" or "province." In this context, "province" seems appropriate. The Japanese had been exposed to European wine since the late sixteenth century.

23 *Shisetsu*: An herbal pill used against fevers.

24 Chen Tsang-chi: A physician from the T'ang dynasty.

25 *Matcha*: Powdered tea used in the tea ceremony.

26 *Sencha*: Regular leaf green tea.

27 The calendar during Ekiken's time was the lunar calendar. The first month began sometime between January 20 and February 19; the year was divided into twelve months, each with either 29 or 30 days.

28 *Kososan*: A mixture of mainly licorice, beefsteak plant, sweet grass, ginger, and dried orange peel. Considered very effective for colds.

29 *Fukankin shokisan*: A mixture of dried orange peel, beefsteak plant, fragrant

pulse, sweet grass, and other plants. Considered to be effective against fevers.

30 Ekiken is probably referring to the *Ch'a Ching* by Lu Yu of the T'ang dynasty.

31 Tensho period (1573–92), Keicho period (1596–1615).

32 That is, introduced by Europeans. Actually, it is probably a West Indian Taino word, signifying the pipe with which the plant was smoked.

33 The kanji—煙草—mean "smoking grass." Although this combination of kanji would properly be pronounced "*enso,*" the Japanese make an exception here.

34 *Roto:* Also called *omirukusa.* Perhaps *Scopola japonica Maxim.* Apparently used as an eye medicine.

35 See Note in the Preface.

36 Pure and essential *ch'i* (精気): Literally "pure or spiritual *ch'i.*" Is this spiritual essence? Sperm, as some writers would have it? Or sexual energy? It would seem to be a form of *ch'i* that is absolutely necessary for both the transmission and the sustenance of life.

37 *Uzubushi* (烏頭附子): A medicinal drug containing wolfbane—*Aconitum chinese* or *japonicum*—used for a number of complaints.

38 *Ta Sheng-lu:* The *Records on Longevity.*

39 The *tanden* (Chinese, *tan t'ien,* literally meaning "field of cinnabar") is located about three finger widths below the navel. According to traditional Chinese medicine and martial arts, it is the place one concentrates one's strength to sustain health, courage, and balance. One strengthens the *tanden* through various exercises, including zazen. This practice is important for the martial arts, Noh, and other arts, as well as for everyday health and to concentrate the mind. Strengthening the *tanden* is very important to the proper circulation of *ch'i,* and it is considered the body's center of gravity.

40 The sage: Here meaning Confucius.

41 Camphor is *ryuno* and musk is *jako.* The former was used for eye disease and toothache, while the latter was used as a stimulant.

42 *I Hsueh Ju Men:* A Ming-dynasty medical book written by Li T'ing.

CHAPTER 3—Foodstuffs

1 See Chapter 2, Note 2.

2 Turnip: *Brassica japonica.*

3 Raw fish and *namasu:* A salad of raw fish and vegetables seasoned with vinegar.

4 *Makuwa'uri:* A melon, *Cucumis melo,* var. *makuwa.*

5 *Nashi:* The Japanese pear. Round and crisp like an apple, and brown in color, it has the aroma of a pear.

6   *Konnyaku*: A hard, gelatinous food made from the bark of the devil's tongue.

7   Knotweed: *Polygonum caespitosum* var. *laxiflorum*. Or, possibly, *Polygonum aviculare*.

8   *Sansho*: Japanese pepper, *Zanthoxylum piperitum*.

9   *Tamari*: Sauce made from refined soy.

10 *Takiboshi*: When the top has not been skimmed off thin rice gruel halfway through the cooking process.

11 *Futatabi'ii*: Cooking rice twice.

12 *Yudori'ii*: Using a lot of water to boil rice, and then steaming it.

13 An Edo-period practice.

CHAPTER 4—Thoughts on Overeating and Treatment for Various Illnesses

1   *Jingi* (参一): Not in any dictionary, but perhaps some form of ginseng.

2   Fluffy cooked: One modern Japanese version gives this footnote: "Fluffy cooked" means steaming an egg with such things as "*irizake.*" The *Kokugo daijiten* defines *irizake* as "stale sake boiled down with soy sauce and dried bonito flakes."

3   *Udo*: *Aralia cordata*.

4   *Shoro* mushrooms: *Rhizopogon rubescens*. Similar to truffles.

5   *Iwatake*: Presumably another kind of edible mushroom.

6   *Matsutake*: *Tricholoma matsutake*.

7   *Yugao*: A kind of bottle gourd.

8   The six beasts: the horse, cow, sheep, dog, pig, and fowl.

9   Kao Shih-lang: Also Kao Yi, an official during the T'ang dynasty.

10 Fan Chung-hsuan: Also Fan Shih-jen, a politician of the Northern Sung dynasty.

11 *Sogoen* (蘇合円), *enreitan* (延齢丹): Both first aid medicines.

12 See Chapter 2, Note 7.

13 This term is not clear. It may mean leakage (of *ch'i*), vomiting, or diarrhea.

14 *Cheng Ch'uan Tsai Wen*: Part of a medical book written by a Ming-dynasty doctor.

CHAPTER 5—The Five Officials

1   *Ping Yuan Hou Lun*: Written by a doctor, Ch'ao Yuan-fang, of the Sui dynasty.

2   *Shou Yang Ts'ung Shu*: A book on nurturing health published during the Ming dynasty.

3   *Doin* (導引): Literally "leading and pulling," this is a Taoist method of health

preservation involving the drawing of *ch'i* through the entire body, thus pacifying the mind and controlling desires.

4 Recall that Japanese sat directly on a straw-mat floor, or with only a thin cushion underneath them. The proper way of sitting was (and still is) with the lower part of the legs tucked underneath the thighs. This is not an easy position to maintain. Martial arts practitioners will understand this.

5 *Liu Ch'ing Jih Cha*: A Ming-dynasty book of essays.

6 *Aitai*: Literally "clouds drifting together in thick array" and, by extension, dark.

7 Arbutus: Also called the "strawberry tree," it is an evergreen tree or shrub with red or yellow berries that have narcotic properties.

8 *I Shou*: A book written by Chang Kao, a doctor during the Sung dynasty.

9 A *kotatsu* these days is constructed as the frame of a low table. A blanket or comforter is placed over the frame, and a table top is placed over the blanket. There is a heating element attached to the underside of the top of the frame, which is then plugged into an electric outlet. A small control sets the heat. In winter, the entire family often sits around the *kotatsu*, with everyone's legs under the blanket. The legs are thus warmed, but not much else.

10 Disorder between blood and *ch'i*: The text has "*kiketsu no fujun.*" A modern translation just puts quotation marks around "*kiketsu,*" as if sort of giving up. The *Kokugo daijiten* defines "*kiketsu*" as "physical *ch'i* and blood; or, the circulation of *ch'i* and blood." When I called up my friend Dr. Justin Newman, a doctor of Oriental medicine, and asked him about this, he said, "Blood carries the *ch'i*, and *ch'i* moves the blood. So if *ch'i* is stuck or obstructed, it affects the blood; and if blood is stuck or obstructed, it affects the *ch'i.*"

11 Tsang-chi: A physician of the T'ang dynasty.

CHAPTER 6—Disease, Your Doctor, and the Art of Medicine

1 Shao K'ang-chieh: A scholar of the Sung dynasty.

2 *Tangyaku*: An illness involving fevers and the overproduction of sputum.

3 The old Japanese calendar was based on the lunar cycle. The New Year generally took place in late January or early February (in the Western calendar), and this was the beginning of the First Month, or in Japanese, the First Moon. The next eleven months followed accordingly. This system required an intercalary month every three years or so to keep the New Year from falling a month ahead of time.

4 *Hsu Han Shu*: A book concerning the history of the Later Han dynasty written by Sze-ma Piao of the Western Tsin dynasty (265–317).

5 See Introduction, Note 8.

6 The Five Elements (五行): Metal, wood, water, fire, and earth.

7 Doctors of Fortune: Perhaps like "Soldiers of Fortune."

8 Mind (意): This character is slightly different from the usual character for "mind" (心), although in this case it is pronounced the same. 意 includes the nuances of attention, interest, care, and intention.

9 See Chapter 1, Note 10.

10 Original purpose (本意): See Note 8.

11 *Li Chi*: The *Book of Rites*, one of the ancient Confucian classics.

12 *Pen Ts'ao* (本草): The fundamental medical herbs.

13 Literally a "grass doctor" (草医), one who is shoddy, unseemly, or incompetent.

14 Shinkei Hoshi (1406–75). A poet and teacher of linked verse.

15 The sage: Confucius.

16 The *Analects*: 2,13.

17 See Note 12.

CHAPTER 7—The Use of Medicine

1 Li K'ang-tzu: A retainer of the state of Lu.

2 *Analects*: 10,12. "K'ang-tzu sent him some medicine. Confucius bowed deeply, received the gift and said, 'As I do not yet have an understanding of this medicine, I cannot take it.'"

3 *Analects*: 2,13.

4 *Jukkan*: *Atractylodes japonica*. Used in Chinese medicine to strengthen the stomach and cause perspiration.

CHAPTER 8—Sustaining Old Age

1 Chu Hsi (1130–1200). The great Confucian scholar whose influence on the people of China, Korea, and Japan was nearly as great as that of Confucius and Mencius.

POSTSCRIPT

1 In the original edition, Ekiken signed his book "Kaibara Atsunobu." The literal translation of the full signature in *Yojokun* is "the eighty-four-year-old Old Man, Kaibara Atsunobu." He signed the same name in another of his works, the *Yamato Zokkun*, but signed "Ekiken Kaibara Atsunobu" in other books. It is unclear why he used different names at different times. "Ekiken" was his professional name.

BIBLIOGRAPHY

Works in Oriental Languages

Daigaku-Chuyo. Shimada Kenji, ed. Tokyo: Asahi Shimbunsha, 1967.

Ekkyo, Vol. 2. Edited and arranged by Takada Shinji and Goto Motomi. Tokyo: Iwanami Bunsho, 2004.

Kaibara Ekiken. *Yojokun*. Ito Tomonobu, ed. Tokyo: Kodansha Gakujutsu Bunko, no date given.

Kaibara Ekiken. *Yojokun*. Sugi Yasusaburo, ed. Tokyo, Tokuma Shoten, 1968

Kaibara Ekiken. *Yojokun-hoka*. Translated into modern Japanese by Matsuda Michio. Tokyo: Choukoron-shinsha, Inc. 2005.

Kaibara Ekiken. *Yojokun-Wazoku doshikun*. Tokyo: Iwanami Shoten, 1961.

Kaibara Ekiken. *Kogo Yojokun*. Translated into modern Japanese by Matsumiya Mitsunobu. Tokyo: Nihon Hyoronsha, 2000.

Kannon-kyo. Oyagi Makoto, ed. Tokyo: Oyagi Kobunto, 1935.

Resshi. Kobayashi Nobuaki, ed. Tokyo: Meiji Shoin, 2004.

Rongo. Kanaya Osamu, ed. Tokyo: Iwanami Shoten, 1963.

Roshi-Soshi. Fukunaga Mitsuji and Kozan Hiroshi, eds. Tokyo: Chikuma Shobo, 2004.

Works in English

Chan, Wing-tsit. *A Source Book in Chinese Philosophy*. Princeton: Princeton University Press, 1963.

Chevallier, Andrew. *Encyclopedia of Herbal Medicine*. New York: DK Publishing Inc., 1996.

Confucius. *The Analects of Confucius*. Trans, by Simon Leys. New York: W.W. Norton & Company, 1997.

Fukuda Masanobu. *The One-Straw Revolution*. Rodale Press, 1978.

Issai Chozanshi. *The Demon's Sermon on the Martial Arts*. Translated by William Scott Wilson. Tokyo: Kodansha International, Inc., 2006.

Hung Ying-ming. *Saikontan*. Translated by William Scott Wilson. Tokyo: Kodansha International, 1985.

Lock, Margaret M. *East Asian Medicine in Urban Japan*. Berkeley: University of California Press, 1980.

Ohnuki-Tierney, Emiko. *Illness and Culture in Contemporary Japan*. Cambridge: Cambridge University Press, 1984.

Tsunoda, Ryusaku; de Bary, William Theodore; Keene, Donald, ed. *Sources in Japanese Tradition, Vol. 1*. New York: Columbia University Press, 1958.

Tucker, Mary Evelyn. *Moral and Spiritual Cultivation in Japanese Neo-Confucianism.*

INDEX

（英文版）養生訓 Yojokun

2008年9月　第1刷発行
2009年2月　第2刷発行

著　者　　貝原益軒
英　訳　　ウィリアム・スコット・ウィルソン
発行者　　富田　充
発行所　　講談社インターナショナル株式会社
　　　　　〒112-8652 東京都文京区音羽1-17-14
　　　　　電話　03-3944-6493（編集部）
　　　　　　　　03-3944-6492（営業部・業務部）
　　　　　ホームページ　www.kodansha-intl.com

印刷・製本所　　大日本印刷株式会社

落丁本・乱丁本は購入書店名を明記のうえ、講談社インターナショナル業務部宛にお送りください。送料小社負担にてお取替えします。なお、この本についてのお問い合わせは、編集部宛にお願いいたします。本書の無断複写（コピー）、転載は著作権法の例外を除き、禁じられています。

定価はカバーに表示してあります。

Printed in Japan
ISBN 978-4-7700-3077-1